THE PROFITABLE ANSWERING SERVICE

---

65 ACTIONABLE STRATEGIES TO BOOST PROFITABILITY, MASTER TECHNOLOGY, AND OUTPACE THE COMPETITION

CALL CENTER SUCCESS SERIES

BOOK 4

PETER LYLE DEHAAN

The Profitable Answering Service: 65 Actionable Strategies to Boost Profitability, Master Technology, and Outpace the Competition

© 2025 by Peter Lyle DeHaan

Book 4 of the Call Center Success Series

Library of Congress Control Number: 2025920137

Published by Rock Rooster Books, Grand Rapids, Michigan

ISBNs:

- 979-8-88809-164-7 ebook
- 979-8-88809-165-4 paperback
- 979-8-88809-166-1 hardcover
- 979-8-88809-167-8 audiobook

Credits:

- Developmental editor: Julie Harbison
- Copyeditor: Robyn Mulder
- Cover design: Cassidy Wierks
- Author photo: Jordan Leigh Photography

To my friends and colleagues in the telephone answering service industry

Series by Peter Lyle DeHaan

Call Center Success Series: Join call center veteran Peter Lyle DeHaan, PhD, as he shares a lifetime of industry experience to help readers operate their contact centers with increased effectiveness, produce greater success, and generate long-term profitability.

Sticky Success Strategies: In the Sticky Success Strategies series of career development books, Peter Lyle DeHaan, PhD, breaks down key business strategies in a coherent, story-driven process to highlight what works and what doesn't. Through personal stories and eye-opening insights, he shares how readers can more effectively produce long-term results and increase their workplace fulfillment.

Be the first to hear about Peter's new books and receive updates at peterlyledehaan.com/newsletter.

CONTENTS

SALES AND MARKETING

OPTIMIZATION

WEBSITE

MINDSET

THE VENERABLE
TELEPHONE ANSWERING
SERVICE INDUSTRY

1

A CENTURY OF INNOVATION

A ROBUST INDUSTRY SPRINGS FROM HUMBLE BEGINNINGS

Today's telephone answering service (TAS) traces its start back to the early 1920s. What it looked like then bears little similarity to what it looks like now. The one consistency throughout its century-long history is people answering phone calls for other people.

Though some automation can minimize or replace the use of people answering phones, the truth remains that most callers prefer to talk with a person and not a computer. Even so, most everything about this fast-paced industry revolves around the telephone.

For the optimist, the TAS industry is rewarding, interesting, and satisfying. Yet the pessimist views it as time-consuming, exhausting, and borderline profitable. Both assessments are accurate.

The people—owners, managers, and frontline staff—who have remained for years, and even decades, see the industry from a glass-half-full perspective. In contrast, many of those with a glass-half-empty viewpoint often leave the industry for more promising opportunities.

Regardless of your assessment of the industry and your plans, this book will give you success tips to move forward positively, coming closer to embracing the industry's dynamic pull on all who remain part of it.

Moving Forward: Commit to embrace the positive aspects of the TAS industry, especially on those days when the negative parts wear you out and try to push you down.

2

CELEBRATE THE TELEPHONE

THE TAS INDUSTRY CENTERS ON A READILY UNDERSTOOD, UNIVERSAL, AND RELIABLE TECHNOLOGY

Telephone answering services handle thousands of phone calls every day. The majority are incoming calls that come from clients' customers and prospects. Most of the rest are outgoing calls made for clients.

With the continued use of the telephone at work, it's easy to dismiss it as commonplace, even boring. But let's not overlook the all-critical role the telephone plays in our everyday work. Let's take a moment to celebrate the telephone as the essential star it is. Let's take time to applaud the telephone.

It's Understood: Everyone knows how to use a telephone. Even those who prefer not to call someone and seek alternative means whenever possible still possess the knowledge of how to call a telephone number and talk to someone.

The telephone is the best understood communication option available. The phone is also the easiest to use and requires little technical expertise and minimal training.

It's Universal: The telephone is also ubiquitous. Though few residences have a telephone sitting in their homes, as they once did, virtually all businesses have a phone—in some form.

Most everyone carries a telephone in their pocket. They may even have two.

Reliable: Email messages may get blocked, end up in spam, or be accidentally deleted. Text messages can suffer delays or non-delivery. Social media posts can get buried and easily overlooked.

Not so with a telephone. A phone call goes through most every time. And in those rare cases when it doesn't, the caller immediately knows by receiving a busy signal or a recording alerting them of a problem.

Moving Forward: It may seem silly to celebrate the telephone, but without it you wouldn't be in business. Though it's easy to overlook the telephone for its always-available, always-working nature, let's pause to appreciate it as the essential element and central icon that it is.

The TAS industry exists because of the telephone.

3

KEY FACTS THAT NEVER CHANGE

FOUR CORE TAS TRUTHS

S ince its beginning a century ago, every year has brought changes to the telephone answering service industry. And the scope of transformation seems to increase each year.

Not everything, however, changes. Some things stay the same. Though these four core truths may fluctuate in importance from year to year, they're always at the forefront of your efforts to provide answering services to organizations and individuals.

1. Timely Communication: You exist because there is a need to respond quickly: to answer the phone as soon as possible and provide information to callers when and how they need it.

2. Professional Service: You represent each client, and they expect you to be professional. Whether it is part of the time or all of the time, you're their public-facing image.

3. Personal Touch: Around 1999, the need for personal touch fell into question in some circles, believing that self-service and automation would surely prevail. That didn't work out so well; a backlash occurred. When self-service and automation fail, people are the answer—every time.

4. Cost-Effectiveness: Although telephone answering services vary in their billing strategies from low-cost provider to premium boutique, the common factor is that you're a fraction of the cost of your clients hiring a full-time receptionist. This means your service is cost-effective when compared to other personal answering options.

Moving Forward: Yes, there are changes afoot, ranging from technology to staffing to legal to financial, but what remains are four keys: timely communication, professional service, personal touch, and cost-effectiveness. Never lose sight of this reality.

MANAGEMENT

4

CUSTOMER COMMUNICATIONS 101

SHARPEN YOUR FOCUS ON WHAT MATTERS MOST

Telephone answering services face a myriad of challenges. These range from competing options to technological solutions, from cost-effective service offerings to ensuring profitability. As a result, it's easy to lose sight of the basics.

Here are the key considerations of Customer Communications 101:

Answer 24/7: The first element is to answer the phone when people call. This may seem obvious, but too often it's overlooked. The point is that when people call, they expect someone to answer. It's that simple.

Yet it's expensive to staff round-the-clock telephone coverage for most businesses. This is the key reason telephone answering services exist. Whether a business receives one phone call after hours or many, each caller deserves the courtesy of having their call answered. Never forget this.

Tap People Not Technology: Building on this essential need to answer calls 24/7 is the need for the personal touch of a human being instead of the impersonal assault of a computer. This stands as the second element in Customer Communications 101.

When customers call a business, their first hope is to have their call answered. Their second concern is who or *what* answers it. This people-over-technology principle will stand until it reaches the point when technology can do a better job than people, performing it faster and with greater accuracy.

Telephone answering services have built their business around this ideal of providing a personal connection to callers. Businesses that force customers to use technology risk losing business just to save a few pennies.

Focus on Caller Satisfaction: The third element is to focus on caller satisfaction. This means successfully addressing the reason for the call. Do it on the first call and do it correctly.

With a needed focus on efficiency, this is the hardest element for a telephone answering service to address. Though it's wise to look at statistical results, don't focus on average call length or number of calls per hour. Pushing to decrease the first one or increase the second are both detrimental to the paramount need of focusing on caller satisfaction.

Provided that you're not wasting their time, callers will seldom grumble about the length of their call, but they're quick to complain about calls that accomplish nothing. That's why the right focus is on customer satisfaction.

Moving Forward: To provide what matters most to callers, pursue three key objectives: answer around the clock, provide a human touch, and focus on satisfied callers. Do this, and you'll make your service indispensable.

5

TECHNOLOGY VERSUS PEOPLE

HIRE STAFF WITH AS MUCH CARE AS IN ACQUIRING TECHNOLOGY

Technology is exciting—at least to me. I love technology and its application. The industry talks a lot about the technology used to help telephone answering services function more effectively and provide a greater array of services to clients. It's hard to imagine processing calls without technology.

Yet without staff, the best technology means nothing. Though the technology in your TAS is critical, the staff who use it are even more important.

When you analyze your operation, it's not your technology that makes you unique; it's your staff. Other answering services can match your technology: computer for computer, application for application, and feature for feature. But no one can match your staff.

Yet the emphasis at too many answering services is on their technology. These operations carefully investigate the options and pick the best one. They implement the technology, train their staff how to use it, and form marketing campaigns to reach a quick payoff for their investment and then generate a profit.

All the while, the staff at too many answering services get whatever attention is left over, which often isn't enough. Too frequently, agents seem expendable. Hire them, train them, and fire those who don't work out.

Too many answering services have an embarrassingly high level of employee churn. Hire ten to find five good ones, one of which may work out for the long term. Frankly, some operations would view those numbers as good, but they're not.

Working at an answering service is hard. Not everyone can do it. And some who could, don't care to. The key is to discover this before hiring them, not after training them.

Just as you'd never buy ten apps and hope one would work out for the long term, you shouldn't accept this when hiring staff either.

Moving Forward: Stop accepting high employee churn as normal. Your employees are your strategic advantage. Reimagine your staffing practices to reflect this reality.

6

COMMON MISTAKES WHEN RUNNING A TELEPHONE ANSWERING SERVICE

DON'T LET THE DAILY PRESSURES OF RUNNING YOUR TAS PUSH ASIDE WHAT MATTERS MORE

R unning a telephone answering service is a challenging proposition. It seems there's always too much to do and not enough time to do it. Therefore, it's understandable when the day ends before you complete your to-do list.

But that's not justification for making these common TAS mistakes.

Allowing Training Shortfalls: It's critical to get new hires answering calls and being productive as soon as possible. Yet too often the temptation is to rush through training. Don't do this. It's shortsighted. Instead, provide thorough agent training to ensure they're ready to handle client calls efficiently and professionally.

Having Inconsistent Processes: Review your standard operating procedures (SOP). Efficiency requires consistent handling and processing of client calls. Every deviation is a chance for an error to occur. Having standard processes in place helps ensure consistent call handling and accurate message taking.

Overlooking Basic Agent Skills: Don't forget the importance of call etiquette and customer service skills. It's the foundation for providing an exemplary service and having satisfied callers. This starts with standard communication skills and proper call etiquette. This is an essential step in providing a positive experience for callers.

Skimping on Technology: Another common mistake is over-looking the importance of having technology that facilitates agents and their work. This doesn't mean you need the latest, leading-edge tools in your answering service, but don't skimp on them either. Keep abreast of the latest developments to determine the right time to invest in technology.

With the right infrastructure in place, you'll increase agent efficiency and enhance customer service outcomes. This will provide a better overall service experience.

Ignoring Data: Answering service platforms generate a plethora of statistics. It's easy to let all the numbers and quantitative output become overwhelming, which leads to ignoring everything. Yet the other extreme is spending too much time dwelling on the numbers.

It's essential to monitor and analyze call data. There are three areas to address: agent metrics, client results, and overall service performance. Don't neglect any of them.

Use the data to make informed decisions to improve outcomes.

Withholding Feedback: Ensure that your agents know how they're doing. Most of them want to do their jobs well and seek ways to improve. And if they don't want to improve, why are you employing them? Give them regular feedback on their performance. This includes both quantitative numbers and qualitative coaching.

By providing ongoing feedback, you'll improve staff performance and enhance service quality.

Forgetting the Client: The function of a telephone answering service is to answer calls for a business or company. Therefore, it's easy to focus on the calls that come into your operation. While you don't want to overlook callers, remember that it's ultimately your clients you must keep happy. Focus on them.

Yes, this starts with keeping their customers happy when they call and serving them with excellence. But as you strive to delight clients' customers when they call, it's possible to overlook your clients.

Assuming Emergencies Won't Occur: A final consideration is to plan for the unexpected. Have a backup plan in place to address unexpected events such as technical problems, staffing shortages, weather issues, natural disasters, local emergencies, and pandemics. Not having an adequate response during a crisis will damage your reputation, frustrate clients, and fail your clients' customers.

When you address these common TAS mistakes, you'll see much of the rest of your operation fall into place. Though these eight issues may seem like a formidable list to deal with amid the day-to-day challenges of running your operation, it's essential to address them. Your job—and the jobs of everyone who works for you—is at stake.

Moving Forward: Don't ignore these common mistakes. Doing so will damage your bottom line and jeopardize the long-term viability of your telephone answering service.

7

MAKE YOUR BILLING STRATEGY WORK FOR YOU

ALIGN TAS RATES WITH OPERATIONAL PARADIGMS

There might be as many TAS billing plans as there are answering services. It seems everyone has his or her own idea of the right way to bill clients, with each answering service viewing its method as superior. Yet privately, they comprehend their method's shortcomings.

In truth, there's no perfect billing philosophy and no single right way to charge clients. Successful billing requires understanding your selected rate structure and adjusting operations to capitalize on your billing structure's strengths and minimize its weaknesses.

Here are some typical TAS billing plans:

Flat Rate: Every client is billed the same fixed rate every month. Though not used much anymore, it was common when client expectations were uniform and call-processing systems were manual.

Advantages: Bills are easy to generate, explain, and understand; all revenue is fixed; and clients know exactly what to expect and can budget accordingly.

Disadvantages: It isn't fair. Essentially half of the clients are profitable, subsidizing the other half who aren't. It also attracts high-volume (unprofitable) accounts while discouraging low-volume (profitable) ones.

Possible abuses: Revenue stays the same regardless if work is done. Therefore, there is no direct financial incentive to answer calls.

Strategy: Seek low-volume accounts. Streamline and automate high-volume accounts.

Modified Flat Rate: Each client pays a flat rate, but that rate differs from client to client based on his or her historical usage.

Advantages: There are the same benefits as with flat-rate billing, and it largely eliminates the disparity between profitable and unprofitable clients.

Disadvantages: Knowing what to bill a new client is hard; it neglects seasonal fluctuations; and you must continually review client traffic for changes in usage.

Possible abuses: The rate for new clients might be too high or too low. Failure to lower rates if usage drops significantly results in elevated bills.

Strategy: Analyze client profitability each billing cycle by calculating client revenue per minute. Clients with a pattern of low revenue per minute (unprofitable) may need their rate increased or their account streamlined and automated.

Unit Billing: Tracks and bills units of work, such as calls answered and calls made; some services charge an additional unit for a message. There is usually a base rate that includes an allowance of units, with excess units being billed additionally.

Advantages: More work can be tracked and billed. High-volume and active accounts pay more.

Disadvantages: Not all units of work require an equal amount of time and effort.

Possible abuses: Performing unnecessary units of work under the guise of being thorough, such as double dispatching.

Strategy: Count every measurable unit of work. Automate time-consuming processes.

Time Billing: The time agents spend working for the client is tracked and billed. As with the unit billing, there is usually a monthly rate that includes a block of time; excess usage is an additional charge.

Advantages: Billing directly reflects the time spent for that client.

Disadvantages: Billing complaints are harder to resolve. Also, the common TAS effort to focus on efficiency and move through calls quickly serves to decrease billable time.

Possible abuses: Talkative agents inflate bills.

Strategy: Provide the client with the services they need; coach agents to be both efficient and thorough; and be sure to track and bill all time.

Tiered Time Billing: Agent time is billed the same way as time billing, and any system time or automated activity is also billed, but at a lower rate. System time includes non-agent activity, such as automated dispatching, call screening, interactive voice response (IVR), voicemail, patching, and conferencing.

Advantages: All the benefits of time billing. In addition, automated activity produces additional income.

Disadvantages: There are more items to track, and not all systems provide adequate statistics.

Possible abuses: The same as for time billing.

Strategy: Be sure to track and bill all appropriate time elements.

Other Billing Considerations: Additional items to be considered are ancillary charges (text, email, or fax delivery; on-call schedules; or handling simultaneous calls), pass-through charges (local, long-distance, and toll-free costs), or surcharges (holiday fees).

Other issues are the length of the billing cycle (monthly versus twenty-eight days), late fees, and discounts for early payment.

Moving Forward: Pick the billing strategy that supports and capitalizes on your operation strategy. Regardless of which method you implement, be sure you know its strengths and weaknesses, follow it ethically, and pursue it strategically.

With the right approach and implementation, any of these methods can be successful.

8

CALL DISTRIBUTION PRIORITY

SHOULD YOU BE FAIR OR PRAGMATIC?

C all me an idealist. I think life should be fair. This applies to answering calls. According to this attitude, call distribution needs to be fair too. This, however, is an idealistic perspective. Answering services exist in the real world and face real issues.

Here are some call distribution schemes to consider:

Equitable Distribution: Everyone has an equal chance of being answered quickly—or at least subjected to the same length of hold time if they need to wait. The call queue would be classless: first in, first out.

Account Types: Equality aside, certain account groups are more important than others. The determining factors vary: client profession, caller urgency, dollar value of the call to the client, type of service provided, or your answering service's specialty.

Chronic Complainers: This results from a natural reaction to the squeaky wheel syndrome. In theory, giving a higher priority to chronic complainers and demanding clients would seem to mitigate their criticisms about service.

Yet for each account you elevate in priority, you effectively demote all others. The account in question receives a more responsive service, which means all others receive a less responsive one. In the end, only half of your clients can receive an above-average response time—and the other half will statistically experience below-average results.

While this strategy seems clever, it's self-defeating to reward clients who complain. And they may be your worst clients in terms of how they treat agents or hassle your customer service and support staff.

Instead, consider giving chronic complainers the *lowest* priority. They're going to complain anyway. When you factor in their drain on customer service resources, they're probably your least profitable clients. If they cancel, you may be better off. (Though I was never brave enough to do this, it might be the wisest move you could make.)

Profitability: What if you assigned call distribution priority based on the profitability of each account?

Here's the logic: at a busy time, some callers are going to hang up; it's inevitable. Which call would you prefer to lose, a call that will bill $2.25 or one worth only $0.49? It's as if two people offer you money: one has a dollar bill and the other a quarter. If you can pick one, which will you choose? The dollar, of course. The same should apply to answering calls: grab the profitable ones first. Don't let them get away.

Even when properly staffed, some callers will hang up before you can help them. It's a fact. So if you're going to miss some calls, wouldn't you prefer to miss the least profitable ones?

If you want to fine-tune this strategy even more, find out who the slow payers and chronic complainers are. Even if they're profitable on paper, they have less value because they hamper cash flow and overuse support resources.

Make sure those calls get answered after the profitable ones. (Full disclosure: I never did this either, but I wish I had.)

Moving Forward: Implement a call distribution strategy that works for you and not against you.

9

EFFECTIVE LEADERS SEEK INPUT FROM EMPLOYEES

INVOLVE STAFF IN DECISION-MAKING

One of my goals when I ran an answering service was to provide the best possible headsets for my staff. After all, they spend all day on the phone, so voice quality, ease-of-use, and comfort are critical.

To pursue this, I always looked for a better headset. When a new model came out that boasted better technology or results, I tested it. Most times, these trial headsets weren't any better than what we already had, so they ended up in a box in my closet, which I later moved to the trash. I would, however, snag the least objectionable one for myself.

Since I used the phone sporadically during the day, headset comfort wasn't a priority. And less-than-ideal voice quality wasn't an issue either. What mattered was that my employees had the best.

After a couple of years, I discovered that my staff had drawn their own conclusions about why my headset differed from theirs. They reasoned I kept the best for myself and forced them to languish with old, subpar units.

At first this upset me. Then I figured out how to set the record straight. I asked a senior agent if she and I could swap headsets for the day. I wanted her opinion on which one was best.

With a smirk, she handed me hers and put on mine. Leaving a smiling agent to do her work, I returned to my office. During her next break, she poked her head into my office. She wasn't smiling. "I don't like this headset—not at all." She shook her head. "The audio's lousy, and the band hurts my head."

"Do you want to switch back?" I asked.

"Yes." She nodded enthusiastically.

Now it was my turn to smile. "My goal is for you and your coworkers to have the best headsets. It doesn't matter what I use, because my work on the phone isn't as important as yours." I paused for dramatic effect. "So, do you think your headset is better?"

She nodded, and I handed her headset back to her. Beaming, she bounced out of my office.

From then on, whenever I tested a new headset, I also checked with an agent before making a final decision. If they liked it, they could use it. And if they didn't, I would. That stopped the grumblings about who had the better headset.

Moving Forward: As an answering service owner or manager, it doesn't matter if you make the right decisions for the right reasons. If your staff doesn't know what you're thinking, they'll likely assume the worst. Communicate with your staff and seek their input.

10

BE CAREFUL WHAT YOU MEASURE
PURSUE THE RESULTS THAT MATTER MOST

A grinning answering service owner marches up to me at an industry convention. "My labor percentage is down to 28 percent," he boasts. "Have you ever heard of anyone lower?" he continues, as though seeking affirmation.

Here's how I wish I had handled it:

"Twenty-eight percent!" I exclaim.

"So, it's good?" he probes, seeking validation.

I contemplate my response. "No, it's terrible!"

"Terrible?" he asks incredulously.

"Yes. Terrible," I confirm. "What are you going to do to fix it?"

"Fix it?" he responds, dumbfounded. "I worked hard to get down to 28 percent. I can't get it any lower."

"It needs to be higher," I state matter-of-factly. After pausing, I clarify. "If your labor is at 28 percent, that implies that your overhead—everything not related to providing service—is at 72 percent. That's way too high and needs to be much lower. I fear your service is suffering from an inflated overhead, and it needs to be brought under control immediately."

A slight glimmer of resigned comprehension forms in his eye, but—wanting to avoid any additional challenges to his entrepreneurial equilibrium—he mumbles a reluctant thanks and makes a hasty retreat.

When answering service leaders focus on labor percentages, they're often looking at the wrong thing for the wrong reason.

Yes, left unchecked, labor costs can quickly escalate, threatening to run out of control. In fact, skyrocketing agent costs are the most likely cause of the *fiscal* demise of an answering service. A too-aggressive reduction of labor costs, however, is the most likely cause of the *quality* demise of an answering service.

Balance cost and quality. Too often, a misalignment sacrifices customer service on the altar of cost-containment.

The Situation: For the sake of illustration, let's imagine a fictitious, yet typical, answering service. To keep the math easy, assume that the answering service has annual expenses of $1 million and spends 50 percent of its budget on agent labor. For simplicity's sake, we'll lump everything else into the broad category of overhead. This assumption is not unjustified, as it is an answering service's labor that directly provides the service, and everything else, albeit important, is ancillary or indirect.

Given this, the answering service's financial picture looks like this:

Expenses: $1,000,000 (100 percent)
Overhead: $500,000 (50 percent)
Labor: $500,000 (50 percent)

So, we have a $1 million answering service, spending $500,000 (50 percent) on labor and $500,000 (50 percent) on overhead. To ensure profitability, costs need to be reduced by 10 percent. Now what?

Scenario 1: According to conventional wisdom, you address the biggest cost area, which is agent labor. Labor is also a variable expense, which means you can reduce it relatively easily. (Fixed expenses are much harder to scale back.) In addition, you'll quickly see the effects of any labor change within a few weeks, whereas reductions in non-labor areas take longer to accomplish.

In any schedule, there are some debatable details. These include the number of agents required at certain times and the length of specific shifts. Even eliminating all these disputable items, there is still considerable—and painful—cutting to do. Eventually, the determined scheduler will make the required cuts, resulting in the target reduction of 10 percent. The annualized results look like this:

Expenses: $900,000 (100 percent)
Overhead: $500,000 (56 percent)
Labor: $400,000 (44 percent)

Accomplishing the targeted 10 percent cost reduction restores profitability, and things are good, right? Not necessarily so. The 10 percent reduction came by cutting agent labor. With overhead remaining unchanged, agent labor itself suffered a 20 percent reduction. This will cause a noticeable drop in customer service levels, both measurably by the answering service and perceptibly by callers. This will produce an increase in complaints, adding work for the supervisory and management staff, while further taxing the agents, who are now working harder than before. It is also likely that some client defections will result, causing income to decrease and the newfound profits to evaporate. This scenario could very well exemplify the adage of "winning the battle but losing the war."

To extend this scenario to reach the overly ambitious goal of 28 percent labor cost, agent labor would need to be reduced an additional $205,556. This results in:

Expenses: $694,444 (100 percent)
Overhead: $500,000 (72 percent)
Labor: $194,444 (28 percent)

Scenario 2: The prudent businessperson may realize the answering service's carefully crafted agent schedule is essentially correct. The agents are the primary determining factor in the quality of service offered and the resulting client satisfaction. Once it has been determined that the agent schedule is on track, the cost reduction efforts can focus on overhead—that is, those activities that do *not* directly affect the provision of quality service.

It's critical to realize that while agent labor is a highly monitored and scrutinized effort, overhead—or non-agent areas—receives less attention and on a considerably less frequent basis. Therefore, these areas are much more likely to be inflated and merit reduction.

Not that cutting overhead is easy. It's difficult, especially since these reductions reside much closer to management. Maybe unneeded perks have crept into the budget; cutting them has no detrimental effect on service. Likewise, other costs are no longer necessary but have continued anyway. Other expenses, left unchecked, have escalated over time and need to be trimmed to a more reasonable level.

Last, there is a labor component in the overhead category as well. This applies to management (at all levels) and support personnel. Maybe a certain position is no longer needed but is kept because everyone likes the person in that job. Other roles could have become bloated with unnecessary tasks or busywork that produces no real benefit to the answering service. Bureaucracy and self-preservation activities are also prime targets for elimination. Finally, there is the possibility that complete departments or management levels might no longer be necessary or at least warrant major reductions.

These types of cost reductions are difficult to make, and they are often harder to spot. Making them, however, has the *least* impact on callers—the very reason your answering service exists. In reducing costs by focusing on areas other than agent labor, the provision of service is not directly affected. The annualized numbers become:

Expenses: $900,000 (100 percent)

Overhead: $400,000 (44 percent)

Labor: $500,000 (56 percent)

The Opposite Extreme: In the first scenario, we looked at reducing the labor percentage. Cutting labor by $100,000 and then by another $205,000, the company realized a 28 percent labor figure.

There is, however, another way to accomplish the same outcome. Holding agent labor constant and *increasing* overhead by $780,000 will also achieve a 28 percent labor figure.

Expenses: $1,785,714 (100 percent)

Overhead: $1,285,714 (72 percent)

Labor: $500,000 (28 percent)

This, of course, is a ridiculous situation, but it powerfully shows the folly of pursuing otherwise well-intentioned goals in isolation.

We see there are two ways to reach a 28 percent labor figure: detrimentally slash labor or obscenely increase overhead. Both cases, however, measure the wrong target for the wrong reason.

Rather, the intent should be to establish an agent schedule that will produce the proper service level to callers and then shrink overhead to the minimal level. This will effectively increase the labor percentage, while decreasing the overhead percentage—a right and worthy goal for any answering service to measure.

Moving Forward: Be sure to pursue the right goals for the right reason and keep them aligned with your service's long-term viability.

11

HOW WELL DO YOU KNOW YOUR ANSWERING SERVICE'S CLIENTS?

A FINAL STORY HIGHLIGHTS A REAL PROBLEM

I once read a novel set in the late nineties. In a small but pivotal part of the story stood a telephone answering service. The author was mostly accurate in describing how an answering service functions, though his depiction of the industry highlighted a few negative stereotypes as the norm.

The FBI investigated one of the answering service's clients, a professional assassin using a fake business as a front. They laid out two options to the answering service's owner: cooperate with us and we will ignore your involvement in your customer's crime, or don't cooperate and face charges as an accessory to over two dozen murders and risk spending the rest of your life in jail.

The owner cooperated. Though she had never met the man who signed up for the service or the woman they contacted with messages, the owner admitted she thought something was suspicious. She assumed her client was involved in some low-level fraud, but nothing to the level of a hitman. Since they paid their bill every month, quickly and reliably, she was willing to ignore whatever business they might be in.

A few days later, her client—the hitman—paid her a visit. The gist of the conversation, aided by the threatening presence of a handgun, was: if you tell the FBI who I am, my associates or I will kill you.

Talk about a no-win situation.

This story, of course, is a work of fiction. But I know that—despite most answering services who carefully avoid working for questionable clients—too many will take any client who can pay. Maybe it's time to rethink that strategy.

Moving Forward: Consider your clients with care. Not every client is a good one. Being able to pay their bill may not be reason enough to keep them.

~

Learn more about business management in Peter's book, *Sticky Leadership and Management.*

STAFFING

12

HOW MUCH DO YOU PAY YOUR ENTRY-LEVEL STAFF?

IT'S TIME TO TAKE A COUNTERINTUITIVE LOOK AT HOURLY PAY

The biggest expense for a telephone answering service is payroll. You know that. You strive to hold down payroll costs to control expenses and stay in business, hopefully to turn a profit. Scheduling too many people to answer phone calls drives payroll costs up. Paying too much per hour also increases expenses.

Left unchecked, runaway payroll costs are the quickest way for an answering service to fail. Or is it? What if you challenged conventional wisdom and dared to consider paying new hires more?

Will It Increase Retention? I've never met anyone at an answering service who felt they earned too much. Most employees, especially entry-level agents, complain they're not being paid enough. I get this—from both the employee and the employer standpoint.

Employees leave an answering service for various reasons. Some quit and exit the workforce, but usually, they leave for a new position —generally one with better pay. And often it's the best employees— the most employable ones—who leave first. Will paying a bit more encourage them to stay a bit longer?

Will It Reduce Other Costs? Assuming that paying telephone agents a bit more increases retention rates, consider the ramifications. If employees stay longer, that means you need to hire fewer replacements. This means hiring costs will go down. Even more significantly, training costs will decrease. You won't have to pay as many new hires for their training, and you'll save on the cost of the trainer.

Will It Improve Customer Service? When you pay an entry-level rate, you get entry-level work. This reflects the level of service your staff provides to your clients. New employees also make more errors. If you pay new employees more, will you get a higher level of work from them? Maybe. Keep reading.

Will It Reduce Management Hassles? Is there a correlation between the level of pay and job commitment? People who arrive late, quit without notice, cause conflicts with coworkers, and trigger a myriad of other issues take up management capacity to deal with. If paying staff more will reduce some of these headaches, is it worth it?

Will It Result in a Higher-Caliber Employee? The fundamental question is, will a higher pay rate result in higher-caliber employees? This is largely up to you. Seriously.

If you pay more but don't change your hiring process or expect more from new hires, you'll realize few benefits by paying a higher hourly rate.

But if you tighten your screening procedures, raise your hiring requirements, and increase your employee standards along with the hourly rate, you can expect to get a higher caliber employee. When you do this, you'll be able to shift money from your hiring and training budget into your operations payroll budget. This could even have a net positive effect on your bottom line.

Moving Forward: Increasing your starting pay to realize these benefits is a high-risk, high-reward proposition. Don't pursue it without careful thought and preparation. However, when done wisely, the result could positively affect every aspect of your answering service.

13

HOW OFTEN DO YOU THANK YOUR ANSWERING SERVICE STAFF?

SEEK EFFECTIVE WAYS TO SHOW APPRECIATION TO FRONT-LINE EMPLOYEES

Where would your TAS be without your staff? Take time to thank your employees for all the work they do to handle your clients' communication needs and keep your business open. Some bosses do a great job at this; others, not so well; and a few don't even think about it.

Here are some ideas to thank your staff.

Use Words: Sometimes the simplest of ways is the best way. Just look each employee in the eye and say, "Thank you for all you do." It can mean a lot.

I once had a boss who personally handed out paychecks each payday. Though not the most personable guy, he made a point of saying "thank you" as he gave each of us our checks. That was decades ago. I still remember it.

Give a Card: Cards are nice, too, but to have maximum impact, don't use the pre-made kind with a flowery sentiment and your printed signature. Instead, handwrite a brief note of sincere appreciation, say thank you, and sign it.

Do Something Special: As the saying goes, "Actions speak louder than words." What action can you take to show your appreciation to your answering service staff working on a holiday, staying late, or going the extra mile?

Maybe you could drop off a treat for them to enjoy during break. How about a small gift awaiting every employee when they come into work? Come up with something creative you can do for your staff, and it will have a huge impact.

Continue Year-Round: Though people think of being thankful during a certain time of year—such as Thanksgiving or Christmas—don't restrict your appreciation of your staff to one day or one weekend. Continue to thank them and show your appreciation for the hard work they do throughout the year.

Moving Forward: Thanking staff takes effort and is time-consuming but even more so is hiring and training new staff when employees quit because they don't feel appreciated.

14

STAFFING LESSONS FROM AN UNLIKELY SOURCE

TIPS FOR FINDING QUALIFIED AGENTS

F inding qualified staff for telephone answering services has always been challenging, but it may be more of a struggle now than ever before. Interestingly, we can gain insights from the food services industry. Before you dismiss the idea, consider that the goal at both restaurants and answering services is to serve people. Also, both industries often tap the same labor pool. What applies to one, readily applies to the other.

My recent experiences at restaurants are most illuminating. They fit into three categories.

The first are restaurants with a quality staff that provide exceptional service. Next are the restaurants whose hiring choices have noticeably slipped in recent years, and their service reflects it. Third are restaurants that can't find enough employees and have scaled back their hours or streamlined their menu and options accordingly.

Which scenario best describes your answering service staffing situation?

Quality Staff: Restaurants in the first category—those with quality staff who provide excellent service—have several things in common. First, they have modern, well-maintained facilities. Their pride in their operation shows. Next, they have accomplished managers and supervisors backed by fine-honed procedures. Third, they offer better compensation packages.

These restaurants don't have "help wanted" appeals hanging in their windows or on their signage. And they haven't lowered their expectations or hiring criteria to find quality employees.

Lowered Hiring Expectations: Restaurants in the second category—those who have lowered their staffing expectations—also have several things in common. Their facilities are acceptable but not much more. They're not as clean as they once were; areas of neglect are apparent. Management and supervision are also lacking, seemingly from decreased expectations and accountability. They have "help wanted" ads in their windows, doors, and signage. They don't pay as much and offer fewer benefits.

Scaled Back Service: Restaurants in the third category— those who scaled back to address their inability to hire staff—are harder to comprehend. The one thing I can identify them having in common is that they seem to have given up on finding enough reliable staff. They act as though being short-staffed is inevitable, and they expect their clientele to deal with it.

One quick-serve restaurant I used to frequent only opens its dining room if enough people show up to work. Otherwise they lock their doors and expect everyone to use their drive-through. As for me, I just drive to the restaurant down the street.

Another area restaurant struggled for months in a downward spiral of being understaffed, having inconsistent hours, and providing inferior-quality food and sub-par dining experiences. They let all their staff and supervision go, starting over with all new employees. These new hires—whom I suspect are being paid more —have restored the level of service this restaurant once offered.

If you lament the poor-quality applicants you receive and struggle to staff as you once did, the problem may not be with the workforce. As hard as it is to say, the problem may be an internal issue.

Moving Forward: Look at your facility, your management and supervision, and your processes. Once these are as good as you can make them, address your compensation package. These elements all work together to bring in the workforce you need to best run your telephone answering service.

15

RETHINKING REMOTE AGENTS

WHAT WAS ONCE OPTIONAL MAY NOW BE REQUIRED

The potential for remote agents to work off-site from the main answering service location goes back to the 1990s. At the time, I addressed this at an industry convention. I covered the two key aspects of having a distributed workforce. One was the technology to make it happen, and the other was managing a dispersed staff.

Technology has changed much since then, with remote access being as simple and as flexible as a good internet connection.

The management concerns, however, remain unchanged. It's still challenging to supervise remotely located employees. Yes, you now have more tools to help you do this, but the human difficulties of managing someone you can't see is still fraught with problems.

Some answering services have avoided remote staff with staunch opposition, while others have pursued—and even embraced—the idea.

For the TAS, the benefits of remote agents are many. These include running multiple offices from one system, tapping new labor markets, and hiring qualified but homebound staff.

For employees, advantages also abound. They include saving money on clothes and eliminating commute time and transportation costs. Of benefit to both are scheduling flexibility—staffing split shifts and short shifts—as well as quickly filling open shifts and responding to traffic spikes.

Often overlooked, though, are the challenges of managing a distributed workforce. It's hard, and some management styles don't work well over distance. There's nothing wrong with "management by walking around," and many use it successfully. But this doesn't translate well to staff you can't see and who can't see you.

I admire managers who successfully oversee staff at multiple locations, yet I also respect managers who decline to try, knowing it's not their strength. But before I let those managers off the hook, I'd like to point out that managing staff at different places is little different from managing staff on different shifts and during times you're not in the office. Take what works for the third shift and apply it to remote agents—things should work out okay.

Given the management challenges associated with not having staff conveniently working in one place has caused many answering services to dismiss remote agents as an option. In other instances, the inability to find and keep a local workforce has driven answering services to embrace remote agents out of necessity.

For many telephone answering services, it's become a matter of survival: go remote or go out of business.

Some who have gone down this path have celebrated the flexibility and embraced it as a new business model, perhaps one even superior to what it replaced: a centralized answering service operation. Other industry leaders, however, look at remote agents as a necessary solution that they one day hope to retreat from. They long for the days of walking into their operation room and seeing all their staff in one place, busy working.

Although having remote agents was once optional, it's now a near necessity, both in the short-term and for future flexibility.

Moving Forward: If you have staff working remotely, embrace it and seek ways to capitalize on it. If you've avoided the idea, open your mind to consider taking a small step in that direction.

16

TIPS FOR MANAGING A REMOTE WORKFORCE

WITH AGENTS WORKING AT HOME COMES THE NEED TO BETTER OVERSEE THEM

Many TAS owners use a management style called "management by walking around." The default method for many entrepreneurs and small business owners, this is a simple yet effective way to oversee a single-location business, provided the manager is on site.

If the manager isn't present, however, the business can quickly degrade. For that reason, absentee owners and telephone answering services with multiple locations or work-at-home agents must embrace another form of management.

Here are some tips for successfully managing a distributed work-force, such as when many employees work from home.

Develop a Remote Perspective: Broadcasting a message to all staff that "there are donuts in the break room" sends a painful message to off-site staff that they don't matter—or you forgot about them, which you probably did. In all your interactions, put your remote staff first. Figure out ways to communicate effectively with off-site employees. Everything that works for remote staff will work for local staff too.

Put All Communications Online: As allowed by law, convert physical bulletin boards to virtual ones. Move from physical inboxes to their electronic counterparts. This may be email, or it may be something else.

Put all necessary paperwork online, making it equally and easily accessible for all staff, regardless of location. The same applies to submitting paperwork. Don't make your remote staff jump through hoops that don't apply to local staff.

Stay Connected: It's easy to interact with office-based staff. This can be as simple as a wave or a head nod when you walk through the operations room. But you can't do this with remote staff. Figure out how to offer the same courtesies to your staff working in their homes. You might periodically want to schedule a video call with them or set up online group meetings. These don't need to be long or complicated interactions. In fact, simple and shorter are better. Aim for quantity over quality.

Update Your Policies and Procedures: A final consideration is to review your written policies and procedures. Make sure they apply equally to local and remote staff. Then, once you have reworded them to be inclusive, post them online, and provide them to each employee electronically. If they need to sign that they received these updates, digitize that process as well. Eliminate the need for printed materials.

Moving Forward: Strive to help remote staff be as successful—and happy—as local staff. This also helps combat the us-versus-them mentality that often occurs between employees who work at different locations.

17

SCHEDULING ANSWERING SERVICE STAFF

PART FACTS AND PART HUNCHES

A lthough you know seasonal fluctuations in call traffic will happen, it's challenging to make the appropriate staffing adjustments at the right time. Even knowing what will occur, many answering services struggle to hire and train enough new staff to be ready to take calls when these traffic increases materialize.

Having the Wrong Schedule: The result of not ramping up the schedule quickly enough is being understaffed, which has two notable side effects. One is that staff is extra busy, and the quality of service suffers, resulting in more complaints and unnecessary cancellations. The other outcome produces increased revenue that isn't fully offset by increased labor costs, which results in increased profits. Ramping up too slowly is both good and bad news: a welcome boost to income coupled with an unfortunate hit to customer service.

The opposite occurs as the season of high traffic winds down. If you fail to anticipate call traffic downturns, the result is overstaffing. This serves to boost the quality of service provided to clients, which disproportionately keeps expenses high at a time when revenue decreases. This produces the opposite outcome of an ill-timed ramp-up.

While these seasonal fluctuations catch new scheduling managers off guard, despite warnings to prepare, even seasoned professionals sometimes fail to react fast enough. Of course, there's always the concern of ramping up staff and not needing them as you move into times of expected traffic increases, as well as scaling back staff but still needing them when you expect to exit the season of higher call volume.

Adjust Sooner and Not Later: Many answering services experience a traffic increase in the summer. This is likely a result of vacations at their clients' offices and those clients using the answering service more. Or maybe they are on summer hours or more of their customers call after hours. Your TAS may have other times of the year when you need to ramp up the schedule. Whatever the reason, the result is more calls into the TAS and increased billing.

When headed into expected times of high traffic, it's best to start hiring and training sooner than you think you need to.

This also means a corresponding jump in payroll to handle the extra calls. (If traffic increases and you don't need to add hours to your schedule, then you were over-staffed to begin with.) The key to adjusting the schedule appropriately is anticipating the need to add hours or staff, not reacting to the changed traffic afterward.

Conversely, begin scaling back staffing schedules when the expected season of higher traffic is anticipated to end, not when the first signs of a decrease occur. If you wait for tangible evidence that call traffic is trending down, it's already too late.

When reacting, the ideal schedule typically lags the actual need by a week or two. This happens both when ramping up to meet increased demand and scaling back in response to decreased traffic. On the front end, this causes understaffing and results in a drop in service quality. On the back end, this causes overstaffing and a drop in profitability.

Though it's ideal to use data to determine your scheduling needs, sometimes it's not possible. The best you can do is guess.

When this occurs, you realize that scheduling staff for an answering service is sometimes more art than science.

Remember Your Staff: Through it all, don't forget your staff. When your traffic projections fail and your staff is busier than you want, it falls on them to bail you out. And they almost always do.

Apologize for your error and thank them for their extra work. And if your schedule was right on target and caused no surprises, thank them anyway. They deserve it.

Moving Forward: Anticipate traffic trends to make sure your schedule moves with traffic changes and the billing tracks with labor costs. Keep service levels consistent so that clients have no added reason to complain.

TECHNICAL

18

DEALING WITH ANSWERING SERVICE TECHNOLOGY

TECHNOLOGY TOOLS CAN BE YOUR FRIEND

M ost telephone answering services use a lot of technology to supplement the work of their agents. Yet technological advances aren't always readily embraced. Though a few visionaries will grasp the application and move forward right away, the other extreme is those who are the last to implement it.

Most people fall in the middle, being neither the first nor the last. They are the cautious ones. Waiting for others to go before them, they only feel comfortable moving forward once they have studied and understand the new technology—whatever it may be. This takes time.

Regardless of where you are on the implementation curve, here are some tips to consider as you evaluate a new technology.

New Technology Evolves: More than once, I've looked at an emerging technology and dismissed it for its lack of utility. My perspective became frozen at that point, and I missed the exciting developments as it evolved. If you've studied promising answering service technology and written it off, it may warrant a repeat look.

Seek a Succinct Explanation: Many people want to fully

understand how an answering service technology works before they'll buy it. Though understandable, this is unnecessary.

When talking with a company about its new product offering, ask for a succinct explanation of what it'll do. Though it may take some effort on the salesperson's part, its essence should be able to be summarized in one or two cogent sentences.

Few people understand how a computer works, yet everyone uses them. The same should apply to your answering service technologies (keeping in mind the next two items on our list).

Know Its Function: Often, marketing people use grand proclamations in promoting their newest product. As you wade through the sales rep's exuberance, you're challenged to understand the essence of their offering.

Here, the goal is to distill into ordinary language what it will do —and what it won't. Don't accept generalities. Insist on specifics.

Understand the Downside: Along with knowing the product's function is understanding its shortcomings. What risk do you open yourself to through this technology? This is often difficult to discover, and vendors are hesitant to acknowledge it.

As you consider the negatives, don't give in to unwarranted fear of the unknown. Instead, ask others what they think. This includes those who have already implemented the new technology, as well as respected and knowledgeable industry technologists.

This will help you be fully informed before deciding.

Implement and Use: Armed with this information, weigh the anticipated benefits and expected outcomes against the acquisition cost and operational downsides to make an informed decision.

If you give yourself the green light, go forth and install the technology in your operation. Don't delay, for this will only minimize its positive impact on your operation.

Moving Forward: Don't blindly embrace a new technology, but don't outrightly dismiss it either. Do your research to make an informed decision at the right time.

19

THE ALLURE OF HOSTED SYSTEMS

SAY GOODBYE TO YOUR PREMISE-BASED SYSTEM

Hosted telephone answering service systems have been around for a long time. Though many operations have praised the benefits of using a hosted system and switched to them, other services have been resistant to make the change.

In contrast to a premise-based system, which you buy, install, and maintain in your office, a hosted system lives off-site and is accessed remotely via the internet. This requires a mental shift from how things have always been to a new way of doing business, but it may be time to embrace that change.

Here are some benefits to consider when looking at a hosted platform to replace your premise-based system.

Financial Advantages: With a premise-based system, you have a sizable capital investment to make, which is a balance sheet item. You must deal with financing and depreciation.

A hosted system is a monthly expense, which appears on your income statement. Check with your tax professional for details, but most answering services realize a financial advantage by going with a hosted system.

Always Up to Date: When you buy an answering service

system, it's expensive to keep it current and running on the latest version. Though some upgrades come at no cost, others may carry an expense. And even with a maintenance agreement, it may not cover some upgrades.

Contrast this with a hosted system, which is always up to date and running the latest software.

Save on Maintenance Costs: A monthly service fee covers system maintenance on a hosted system. There is no need for a maintenance contract or hiring expensive IT personnel. Though you will still have agent terminals to deal with, the room full of equipment and the need to keep it running at all times is gone.

Improved Reliability: The real-time backup systems and the fault-tolerant infrastructure inherent in a hosted system greatly reduces downtime compared to an on-site system. This isn't to say downtime will never occur, because it's a reality with any technology, but it's much less likely than with a premise-based system.

Free Up Facility Space: How large is your equipment room? Imagine tapping that space for other uses. Yes, you will still have some equipment in your office, but it's more likely to fit on a shelf in a closet than take up a full room.

Eliminate Parts Inventory: To minimize downtime with your on-site system, you must maintain an inventory of all critical parts. This is a costly investment that offers no benefit other than to give you peace of mind, with the potential to decrease the length of system downtime.

Slash Telco Costs: With a hosted TAS system, you also cut your telephone costs, as most of that shifts to your provider, as covered by your monthly invoice. Yes, you may still have some office phone lines or an emergency backup landline, but that's minimal compared to your current telephone answering service expenses.

Reduce Utility Expenses: A premise-based system consumes a lot of electricity to run 24/7. When you remove that equipment from your office, you also eliminate that expense. A parallel issue is backup power: a UPS (Universal Power System) and generator. With a hosted system, these can be much smaller or may not be needed at all.

Something that's often overlooked, however, is that your premise-based system generates a lot of heat. This carries with it an air-conditioning cost to dissipate that heat. If you don't keep your equipment room cool, your system will overheat, causing increased downtime and reducing system life expectancy.

Moving Forward: Despite all these benefits, a hosted system deserves thoughtful consideration for your telephone answering service. If you're still unsure, ask someone who's already made the switch.

20

TWO MAIN TYPES OF AI

NOT ALL VERSIONS OF ARTIFICIAL
INTELLIGENCE ARE THE SAME

I hesitate to discuss AI. That's because it's changing so rapidly; anything I say could be out of date before this book comes out. Keep this reality in mind as you read this chapter and the rest of this section.

To first put things in perspective, you don't need to worry about AI making your answering service obsolete. Instead, you need to worry that another TAS using AI will make yours obsolete. Contemplate this.

We'll start with the basics and then build upon them.

There are two types of artificial intelligence. The most recent version of AI is generative AI. Contrast this with predictive AI, also called regular AI, non-generative AI, or analytical AI. For simplicity, we'll refer to all these alternate labels as predictive AI, simply because it's the term more regularly used.

Though both types of AI rely on machine learning, they have significant differences. Here's a basic breakdown of the difference between predictive AI and generative AI.

Predictive AI: The older and more accepted forms of artificial intelligence fall into the camp of predictive AI. As the name suggests, predictive AI predicts responses to what you are doing. It taps a vast database of past results to project future paths.

Some common examples are autocomplete when typing messages or doing online searches. As you type, predictive AI suggests what it deems to be the most likely word or phrase to complete what you've already entered.

Autocorrect—or auto spellcheck—is another common implementation of predictive AI. Predictive AI can also prefill forms or suggest more common phrasing as you type messages.

When appropriately implemented, predictive AI can help telephone answering service staff improve their accuracy and increase their productivity. Yet to be successful, staff must have the ability to override artificial intelligence's predictions, know what to look for, and have the confidence to act.

Generative AI: In contrast to predictive AI, we now have generative AI. This is also based on machine learning and has vast databases to tap into. Yet the distinction is that while predictive AI bases its recommendations on past reality, generative AI produces new content deduced from what it knows.

That is, it generates answers. The quality of what it generates exists on a continuum ranging from highly intuitive to pointedly absurd. In short, its made-up answers can, at times, be laughable and unrealistic, which almost any person can readily determine but a computer cannot.

What becomes even more worrisome with generative AI is when it uses prior AI-generated results as part of its base dataset. This works well when the prior generated content is accurate, but errors quickly compound when it taps faulty conclusions.

Generative AI, by the way, is the basis for science fiction apocalypses, where computers determine that people are a problem and set out to eliminate them.

Though this outcome should cause you to proceed with care before you implement generative AI into your answering service, this is not to suggest a total rejection. Though you may not be ready to trust your business to a generative AI tool, you may one day see the potential to tap it for basic applications. When that day comes, be sure to proceed with care.

Moving Forward: Know that not all AI is the same, with predictive AI and generative AI being distinctly different. Before you consider implementing either of them in your answering service, learn their strengths and their weaknesses, weighing both the rewards and the risks.

21

HOW SHOULD YOU VIEW ANSWERING SERVICE AI?

DETERMINE THE ROLE ARTIFICIAL INTELLIGENCE WILL PLAY IN YOUR TAS

U nless you're intentionally ignoring it, talk of artificial intelligence is hard to miss. AI is not a fad that will fade, nor a hype that will die down. AI is a trend that will continue to grow and become more pervasive in our everyday lives. It's infiltrating every industry, including telephone answering services. Given this, you may wonder how to view answering service AI.

Let's set aside the doomsday prognosticators who foresee a future where artificial intelligence will take over the world and deem human life as inadequate and worthy of eradication. Though some futurists view this as a slim possibility, there's little you or I can do to stop it. And the degree to which you embrace or dismiss AI will have no bearing on the technology's overall impact.

Therefore, instead of fearing the concept of AI on a macro level, consider the potential of AI on the micro level, such as at telephone answering services. Given this, how should you view answering service AI?

AI Is Not Something to Fear: First, there's no need to be afraid of using artificial intelligence in your answering service. Though you may not understand how AI works to do what it does, you don't need to. What you need to focus on is the result, the outcome the technology provides. The how doesn't matter.

AI Is a Tool: Next, view AI as a tool. Just as a computer is a tool, the internet is a tool, and VoIP (Voice Over Internet Protocol) is a tool, so is AI. In the same way you evaluate the cost, the effectiveness, and the outcome of any tool you acquire for your answering service, do the same with AI.

Can you afford AI? Will AI be effective? What results will AI provide? If the answers to this deliberation are positive, then look to add this tool to your toolbox.

Note that AI is not one application, but a way to empower *every* application. This means you will end up with multiple AI-powered tools in your answering service.

AI Should Be a Strategic Consideration: As with every other business decision, tapping AI for your answering service should be a strategic choice. Don't jump on the AI bandwagon without first considering its risks. Don't let FOMO (fear of missing out) rush you into a rash decision. Instead, craft an informed judgment based on facts and a careful cost-benefit analysis.

Moving Forward: Using artificial intelligence in your answering service may be ideal for your operation and goals. Conversely, it might not be the right solution for you at this time. But don't dismiss it without first considering it. The only wrong approach is to ignore it.

22

APPLYING AI IN TELEPHONE ANSWERING SERVICES

CONSIDER THE ROLE ARTIFICIAL INTELLIGENCE COULD PLAY IN YOUR TAS

Not only will artificial intelligence revolutionize business and the answering service industry along with it, but it will reach into and touch every aspect of our lives. In fact, it's already doing just that, whether or not you know it.

Here are some ways you might apply AI to your telephone answering service.

Supplement Management and Support: AI can function in a support role, assisting the functions and departments that surround your telephone answering service operation. Already, AI is great at producing the first draft of an email or suggesting attention-grabbing subject lines. The same applies to marketing materials and ad copy. Don't expect AI to make a perfect final draft—at least not yet—but those days are coming, and they'll likely arrive sooner than you expect.

Look for other ways AI can assist non-operation departments, such as accounting, sales, marketing, and technical. These AI tools are ready today or are close to being ready. All you need to do is find and implement them.

Enhance Customer Service: The same applies to customer service functions. If a concern arrives via email, AI can often make the first draft of a cogent response. All you need to do is verify and tweak.

Chatbots are another area. You've likely had experience with them, albeit on the user side. Imagine what AI chatbots can do for your customer service. But before you get carried away trying to implement a comprehensive system that will cover everything, start simple and address the basics. Once that's working fine, expand it.

Another area related to customer service is tapping AI to perform agent evaluations. This isn't just for select calls or random ones but for every call. Only outlier results needing attention— either to correct an error or celebrate a success—need to be forwarded to the agent or management. [Learn more in Peter's book, *Sticky Customer Service*.]

Better Handle Calls: Most of the work—and most of the labor—at an answering service occurs in the operations room and revolves around answering calls or handling communication for clients. This is where AI can have the biggest impact.

Start by considering how AI can better support your telephone agents to allow them to do their jobs more effectively, quicker, or both. But don't stop there. Also consider service activities you can move to AI, with agent oversight and the ability to overrule. And, of course, there are areas you can completely outsource to AI.

A Tool to Embrace: Some people are technology averse. There's nothing wrong with that; it's who they are. They just need to realize that ignoring AI won't make it go away, and it will one day put their TAS at a disadvantage.

Consider the last services to switch from cord boards to computerized systems. Or the last providers to stop handwriting messages and start entering them into a database. Though there were holdouts—sometimes for quite a while—they eventually realized they had to embrace the technology. So, too, will be the case with AI.

Moving Forward: With artificial intelligence, opportunities abound. They're almost limitless. If you can dream it, it can likely be done—or someone has already done it.

23

MATCH AI TECHNOLOGY TO ANSWERING SERVICE STRATEGY

EMBRACE ARTIFICIAL INTELLIGENCE TO HELP YOU MEET GOALS MORE EFFECTIVELY

I f you're like many people, you might be worried about how artificial intelligence could affect our world, including your TAS. You might fear AI will emerge as a disruptive force that will fundamentally change your day-to-day operations.

It probably will.

But there's no need to fear AI. Instead, embrace it. The key is to align the promise of AI with your business strategy. Tap this burgeoning technology to better accomplish your goals for your TAS operation.

Here are some scenarios to consider.

Basic Service: Some clients are on a budget. They know voicemail won't cut it, but they only need the basics of name, number, and message. They view anything more as frivolous. That's when AI can come to the rescue. At first, this will involve supplementing the work of your staff, with an eventual potential to replace much of their work—but not all.

Low-Cost Service: If your answering service strategy is to be a low-cost provider, AI can be a great tool to help you save on labor costs, while still providing the level of service your clients want, expect, and pay for.

But don't plan on AI replacing your staff. Instead, view it as a tool to help your agents do more in less time and do it better with greater ease.

The result is that AI will help you maintain your low-cost paradigm and maximize it for your clients' benefit.

Premium Service: A third consideration is the value-added approach. Your goal is to offer more than your competition. In the past, the premium service strategy drove up payroll, not only in needing more staff but also in paying them better.

When offering a premium service, however, there comes a point of diminishing returns. At some level, clients will balk at paying more for the extra value. They'll decide it's not worth a higher bill, no matter how much better your service is.

In this instance, you can tap AI to handle supplemental activities that increase the value of your service without growing your payroll. This can be on both the front end and the back end. Use your imagination. Get creative.

These three examples show how AI can effectively help you achieve your answering service strategy in a cost-effective way. But these are just the starting points.

Moving Forward: Develop your ideal service strategy and then look at how AI can help you better achieve it, not the other way around.

SALES AND MARKETING

24

ANSWERING SERVICE MARKETING, THEN AND NOW

SALES AND MARKETING TACTICS CHANGE, BUT THE NEED TO CLOSE SALES DOESN'T

I n the early days of the telephone answering service industry, all clients were local. This was because a physical off-premise extension of the customers' phone line needed to be installed in the answering service. If the client wasn't local to the answering service's office, this was cost-prohibitively expensive.

This meant that hiring an answering service was a local buy. And the only effective competition—if any—was another local provider.

Then came call forwarding, local DID (direct-inward-dial) numbers, toll-free numbers, and toll-free DID numbers. These provided the potential for every answering service across the country to compete with every other answering service. Throughout this, the marketing focus of most answering services remained on their local city.

A subsequent advancement came with VoIP, which completely opened the market. This made every answering service with this technology a competitor to every other service in the country.

Marketing That Worked Then: Some of the common marketing efforts when the focus was on the local community included yellow pages ads, local print advertising, direct mail, direct sales (cold-calling, lead follow-up, or both), networking, word of mouth, and referrals.

Of course, individual results varied, but most answering services found success in one or more of these strategies. These techniques worked well when the focus was on the local market, but they're not so effective when pursuing a broad geographic area.

Marketing That Works Now: When casting a net over a wider geographic region, the common go-to solution is online advertising. The ability to target ads to specific areas and prospects is an attractive option, especially when contrasted with yesterday's broadcast marketing solutions.

Running effective online marketing campaigns is a skill people best learn through doing. Expect to make some mistakes and lose money in the initial stages, but with practice and intention you can run successful online advertising campaigns.

Closing Leads: The goal of marketing is to find prospects, that is, to generate leads. The goal of sales is to close these leads.

For an answering service to grow, it must excel in both aspects of the sales and marketing equation. Just as you track online marketing effectiveness by the number of clicks, you track sales effectiveness by the number of closed deals.

Generating leads is the first step. Closing leads is the second. Both are essential to having an effective sales and marketing campaign.

Moving Forward: To make sales, you first need leads. Start there.

25

TWO WAYS TO GROW YOUR TAS

SALES AND MARKETING VERSUS ACQUISITION

Most TAS owners want to grow their businesses. Even those who want to keep the operation at its present size need to add new accounts to make up for cancellations. To grow your TAS, there are but two ways: through sales and marketing or through acquisition.

Sales and Marketing: Sales and marketing allow for controlled expansion at a steady and manageable rate, without taxing staff or infrastructure. This requires no extra stress or additional work, and other projects aren't put on hold.

Acquisition: Acquisition provides a nice jump in size all at once. A team spirit develops as staff pull together to integrate the new accounts or another location into an existing operation. The effort is intense, and then activity settles into a new normal.

Considering which method best fits your goals is a great place to start. Don't, however, overlook your own strengths. I always desired the methodical predictability of the sales and marketing approach, yet I had trouble finding the right sales staff and managing them to succeed. What I was good at was acquisitions: the pursuit of the deal, the negotiation, and the integration afterward.

Both growth options are legitimate considerations, but don't do what everyone else is doing. Pick the option that works best for you and fits your staff. If you have a strength, go with it. If you have a weakness, work to improve it.

Moving Forward: Determine if your primary growth initiative should be sales and marketing or acquisition. Though you can do both, you'll likely excel at one.

26

CONSIDER CONTENT MARKETING

PROVIDE VALUABLE INFORMATION YOUR CLIENTS AND PROSPECTS WILL APPRECIATE

A blog is a common place for content marketing and a great way to connect with people online. It also provides fresh content, which makes search engines happy. Happy search engines show your site to more people, giving you a higher position in their rankings. This is becoming even more important, with AI looking for—and reporting on—solid industry information.

A well-done blog will drive traffic to your website. If a blog brings more people to your site, it seems like a can't-miss strategy. And it is, provided you can sustain it.

Regularly coming up with good, fresh content challenges most TAS leaders, who are already too busy. If you make content marketing a priority, you want to make it count. Avoid blogging about random topics that don't provide value to your readers. You want to post what matters. This means being strategic.

Vision: Content marketing provides information your audience will appreciate, find useful, and see as beneficial. It isn't advertising; it isn't the place for self-promotion. Your content marketing piece will seldom end with a direct call to action.

Though this will frustrate advertising-focused people, the goal of content marketing is to provide value to readers. In doing so, you establish yourself or your company as a credible source of practical content they'll want to read month after month.

Then, when they have a need you can fill, they'll contact you.

Find a Topic: To guide your writing and direct your vision, you need a theme for your blog. That way, your audience will know what to expect, and you'll meet their expectations every time. What should your theme be? That's a great question.

What are you and your team knowledgeable about? This is an ideal place to start. There are two general areas to consider: answering service content and client-focused content.

For content marketing focused on the answering service industry, you'll certainly be writing about what you know: answering services. Just remember, this is not a place to promote your business. This is a place to provide intelligent and actionable content to help clients better use their answering service or to guide prospects to better understand how to select one.

When you do this honestly, you help everyone who uses or may use an answering service—even if it's not yours—but if this happens, don't despair. Your excellent posts about the industry position you as a go-to expert, and eventually they're bound to go to you.

Frequency: Determine how often you will post. The key is consistency. Once a month is minimum, but once a week is better. Just don't commit to more often than you can handle.

Writing: Decide who will write the posts. Pick people who like to write and have a knack for it. Don't force department heads to each take a turn; nothing good will come from that.

Some companies outsource some or all their content creation to freelance writers or professional bloggers. This is an option, especially if you're struggling for ideas or if you lack time. If you do this, pick someone with a proven record who understands your business, the industry, and your target market.

Another option is to use generative AI to write posts for you. But don't assume this is a one-click-and-done solution. Someone must provide the prompt, evaluate the results, and tweak the output. If you're not careful, readers will subconsciously sense something is wrong with the piece, even if they don't pointedly realize it is AI generated. (In case you're wondering, I never use generative AI to write my books, articles, or blog posts.)

Client-Focused: You can also do content marketing around a topic that's of interest to your clients or a large group of them. Think of this as a value-added service. For example, if you are a medical answering service, cover topics of interest to healthcare practitioners. If you specialize in the service industry, write about that. If most of your clients are small businesses, provide them with valuable information about running their companies.

The Goal: Regardless of the topic you pick, the goal is not to sell your services but to position yourself as a thought leader and earn their trust. Over time, your content marketing pieces will help drive business your way. Even if you have a regular reader who loves what you write but never uses your service, take solace in knowing that your words benefit the industry.

Moving Forward: Everyone wins with content marketing, but don't try it if you're not 100 percent committed.

27

WHERE ARE YOUR CLIENTS LOCATED?

ALIGN SALES AND MARKETING STRATEGIES WITH CLIENT GEOGRAPHIC DISTRIBUTION

Since you can target online ads to specific markets, conduct a geographic analysis of where your customers are located. Let the results inform future ad targeting.

Here are some considerations:

Local Market: Though there's no longer a technical reason to go with a local answering service, some businesses prefer to work with nearby vendors. Their reasons vary, but the major factor is that their preference to buy local gives you an automatic advantage over *everyone else* who's marketing to them from a distance. Use this fact to your benefit when targeting your local market.

Highly Reached Markets: Is there another city or state where you currently have a lot of clients? Explore why. Look for ways to capitalize on these reasons in online marketing initiatives. Another benefit is that when closing the sale, you'll impress some prospects if you can list other businesses in the area you already serve.

Under-Reached Markets: Now consider other states or regions where you have few customers or none. Is there a reason for this? Let this explanation inform your decision about targeting these areas. Maybe you've never marketed in that area. Or perhaps you did, but the results disappointed you. If so, see the next item.

Conduct a Test: Your current geographic distribution of clients is a culmination of past factors, but this may not indicate future success. Therefore, some periodic wide-scale testing is in order.

Conduct an online ad campaign targeting your ideal client, but don't specify any geographic area. Then, look at the results.

If you receive a greater click-through rate in a particular geographic market, this area may be interested—for whatever reason—in switching answering services. It doesn't really matter why. The key is that your message resonates with them right now. So target that area. Continue to do so for as long as you see results.

Time Targeting: I once mused about having an answering service with 25 percent of my client base in each major US time zone. This would smooth out each day's traffic peaks and valleys that occur when most all clients are on the same schedule. With geographic online ad targeting, it's possible to pursue this specific time zone mix—assuming you want to.

Moving Forward: TAS marketing tactics change. A current marketing favorite is online advertising, but this is only half the equation. The other half is sales. Keep reading to learn more.

28

GET MORE CLIENTS

DISCOVER THE KEY CHARACTERISTICS TO CLOSE MORE SALES

The previous chapter talked about identifying where your clients are located and adjusting your marketing strategy accordingly. Now you must close the leads these marketing initiatives uncovered.

People have written and will continue to write much about making sales, but a few key principles establish the foundation for sales success. Sadly, too many organizations fail to address these essential elements and can't figure out why the latest can't-miss marketing initiative isn't producing the results they want.

Here are some commonsense characteristics that too many organizations overlook as they pursue other strategies.

Respond Fast: The first key is to react quickly. Gone is the time when the next business day or within twenty-four hours is good enough. Though some services have a one-hour response goal, even this falls short in today's market where prospective clients seek instant results. Studies abound about response rate efficacy, but the essential truth is the faster you respond to an inquiry, the more likely you are to close a sale.

And to be clear, I'm not talking about the time from when a sales rep gets the lead to when they make the first contact, I'm talking about from when a client clicks a link or submits a request to when they're interacting with a sales professional.

Strive to make this as fast as possible. The goal is to close the sale before your competition even responds.

Follow Up: The second key is ongoing interaction. Most people pursue simple solutions and desire to achieve the best results with the least amount of effort. Salespeople are no different.

It's true that many sales close on the first interaction, with the success rate tapering off with each subsequent follow-up effort. Yet contacts two through ten (or more) produce a substantial number of sales as well.

It's just that most salespeople don't know this because they don't follow up with their leads. They seek the quick sales from those initial contacts and write off the prospects who don't readily say *yes*.

Be Intentional: The next key is to ensure that each contact you make has a purpose. Don't call a prospect to "touch base" or see if they're ready to begin service. Instead, be deliberate with each contact, be it by phone, email, or text. Make sure each interaction moves the sales process forward.

Learn the steps they plan to take to make their decision. Do they need someone to sign off on their recommendation? Do they need to research something? They might need to look at their budget. Ask them how you can help them move the process forward.

Another option is to contact them with additional information. This might not even relate to your answering service or them using it. If you find something applicable to their business or could interest them, that's a great reason to contact them.

The point is that each follow-up contact should move them closer to deciding to use your service.

Don't Stop: The fourth key is persistence. Too many sales-people give up too soon. Know that some people are deliberate in making changes and need time to process it. Don't risk giving up just as they're getting ready to say *yes*.

Continue following up with prospects until there's no more reason to do so.

The most obvious reason is that they sign up to use your

answering service. Another reason is that they tell you to stop contacting them; respect that. And if they've gone with one of your competitors, ask their permission to follow up with them at a certain point to see how things are going.

A timely call could turn a *no* into a *yes*.

Moving Forward: A foundation for sales success is to respond fast, follow up diligently, be intentional, and don't stop. Few salespeople do this. Implementing these four basic tips will put you ahead of most others. This means you'll close more sales.

29

HOW DO YOU USE SOCIAL MEDIA?

VIEW SOCIAL MEDIA AS THE SPOKES OF THE WHEEL AND YOUR WEBSITE AS THE HUB

Most telephone answering services have a website. That's great! But not all do. They don't think it's worth the modest investment and feel social media serves them well enough. I've also heard from services thinking about ditching their websites in favor of social media. That would be a risky move.

Here's why:

Just Because It's Easy Doesn't Make It Ideal: Social media is simple to use. Most of your staff are already adept at using the major platforms. And you likely have a platform-specific expert on staff who could help with any up-and-coming provider you might consider.

This is not the case with websites, which require a bit of expertise to manage and have a cost component, even though it may be small. But just because social media is easy doesn't mean it's the best solution. With social media come significant risks, which you can smartly avoid by having your own website.

The Narrative is Harder to Manage on Social Media: The messaging on social media is challenging to manage—not yours, but everyone else's. Anyone can say anything to anyone about your posts. And too many will. On some platforms you can block these offending messages, but on others you can't. And too often these contrary messages spark an online war between your supporters and your detractors. No one wins.

Nowadays, few websites allow visitor interaction. And for those that still do, you—as the website owner—can delete the offending message. Your website is a safe place with relevant information about your business. You can keep it free of trolls and malcontents.

You Can't Control How Social Media Looks or Functions: The wonderful (and sometimes frustrating) thing about social media is that it has a predetermined format for you to follow. Though you can control what you add, you have little say over where it goes or what it looks like. It offers little flexibility or customization capabilities beyond a few basic options.

Though some website vendors follow this same philosophy, a self-hosted website offers a blank canvas for you or your design team to configure the way you want it and make it function however you wish.

You Don't Own Your Social Media Pages: The most compelling reason to be wary of social media is that you don't own your page on any platform. Your provider does. They can limit who sees your messages. More infuriatingly, they can charge you so that the people who want to see your information actually can.

Even worse, they can summarily shut your account down at any time for any reason, leaving you with little recourse. When this happens, you've lost all the traffic and the audience that you took years to build.

Owning your own website smartly avoids these problems and the chance of you falling victim to the whims of the social media overlords.

View Social Media as a Tool and not a Destination: This isn't to suggest you should avoid social media. But it should be ancillary and not primary. If you use social media, treat it as a spoke on a wheel, using it to point visitors to your website—your online hub—which you own and control.

Moving Forward: If you like social media, go ahead and use it for your TAS. But don't make it your focus. Instead, use social media to point people to your website, the one online destination you own and control.

And if you don't like social media, don't use it. Focus on your website. That's what matters most.

30

HOW TO HANDLE PRICING ON YOUR WEBSITE

POSTING TOO MUCH INFORMATION MAY WORK AGAINST YOU

Over the years I've looked at hundreds of telephone answering service websites. A few are great, many are good, and some need improvement. A common page on many answering service sites covers pricing. There are different ways to handle rate information, each with its advantages and disadvantages.

Post Rates Online: Though I've never tracked it, I think most answering service websites post their rates and rate packages.

The advantage is eliminating budget-conscious shoppers—who won't hire you anyway. But this conditions buyers to shop for price. Remember, if someone selects your service based on price, they'll leave as soon as a better price comes along. High churn results. Therefore, beware of this practice.

Request a Call: Another approach is to encourage people to call you for more information. You could say something like, "Contact us today for a customized package to fit your specific needs."

The advantage of this approach is setting the expectation that you'll design an answering service solution to meet the unique requirements of the prospect. The disadvantage is you invest time pursuing clients who merely want the cheapest rate.

Complete a Form: A step up from requesting the prospect to call you is presenting them with a simple form to fill out to receive more information. Since they're already on your website, this is an easy ask. The fewer questions you require them to fill out, the greater the chance they will complete your form. Know that the more fields you require, the less likely a prospect will complete it.

The advantage of using a form is you'll get more requests for information than if you ask them to call. The disadvantage is even more cost-conscious prospects to weed through.

Use an Online Quoting Tool: A more sophisticated option is an online quoting tool. Prospects enter their basic call parameters and call volume into an app on your website. Have the tool automatically provide a custom quote to best meet their expected usage. You can either display their custom quote once they enter their information or you can automatically email it to them. Getting their email addresses allows you to follow up.

The advantage of using an online quoting tool is that you can still provide rates quickly to prospects, thereby eliminating those who are just shopping for the best price. This also keeps you from posting rates online. The disadvantage is in the cost of setting up the quoting tool and maintaining it.

Moving Forward: Consider the advantages and disadvantages of providing online rate information based on what you want to accomplish, your position in the marketplace, and how your prices compare to those of your competitors.

31

SHOULD YOU LIST MAJOR ACCOUNTS ON YOUR WEBSITE?

BALANCE THE NEED TO PROTECT YOUR CLIENT LIST WITH YOUR DESIRE TO CLOSE SALES

When telephone answering services overhaul their websites or seek to tweak their content, many wonder if they should post a partial list of their major accounts. Some answering services do this, but I have mixed feelings about the practice.

Pros: On one hand, listing major accounts gives credibility to your organization and the services you provide. It lets prospects know that larger companies, whom they respect, have already investigated your services and picked you. What a powerful endorsement.

Cons: Posting your major accounts, however, also tells your competitors who they can target. This gives other services the opportunity to contact your accounts and try to steal their business from you. In an industry noted for its high client churn rates, is it worth the risk of giving competitors a head start on poaching your most valued clients?

Of course, the counterargument is that if you provide great service and high value, you're not in danger of losing them anyway.

Display Logos: Some services that list major accounts will just display client logos. These images, especially of well-known companies, provide immediate credibility to your prospects without opening you to too much risk exposure. The larger the company, the truer this is. Visually, this affords much greater impact than merely listing the company name.

A related issue is whether to link the logo or company name to your client's website. Though your client might appreciate the link for search engine optimization (SEO) purposes, it accomplishes little else.

Post Testimonials: Another approach is to ask for and post testimonials. Some services will list the organization and the person's full name and title. This invites your competitors to approach these clients.

Instead, don't share the person's last name, and maybe not the company name either. Instead, give the industry they're in. This would produce a testimonial tag such as "Julie B., director of communications at a major hospital network."

References Available: A third option is to post nothing online. Instead, note that references are available upon request. This goes a long way in protecting your client list from poaching, while still providing an extra push to help close the sale.

Moving Forward: Before you post your major accounts online for the entire world to see, consider the downside, what you hope to accomplish, and if there's a better way to reach that goal. It's hard work to land a new answering service account, so make sure you do everything to keep them once they sign up.

~

Learn more in Peter's book, *Sticky Sales and Marketing*.

OPTIMIZATION

32

LOOK FOR WAYS TO BETTER SERVE YOUR CLIENTS

SEEK INITIATIVES TO STAND OUT FROM YOUR COMPETITION

You're proud of your telephone answering service, at least I hope you are. This means you strive to serve your clients and their callers well. You do things with excellence. You relish the fact that you facilitate hundreds or thousands of communication efforts every day.

Yet your competitors feel the same way. Every answering service does.

So how can you stand out? What can you do to differentiate yourself from every other service, which seems to be just as impressive as yours?

You should focus on providing quality service, just like everyone else. This isn't a distinguishing factor anymore but an expectation. In addition, look for ways to better serve your clients.

Here are some areas to consider.

Inquiries: The first idea to better serve your clients is to start before they become your customer. One area to look at is the amount of time from when they click on your ad to when they're having an actual conversation with someone on your team. An automated response or AI-powered bot doesn't count. Only true human interaction matters.

Strive to shorten this time as much as possible. Establish proce-dures to aid in this effort and reform your sales staff's perspective of the imperative need to respond right away.

Onboarding: Once you've closed the sale, the next step is setting up their account and being ready to answer calls. Again, measure the time from when they commit—such as submitting paperwork or signing an online form—to when you answer their first call.

Streamline this process as much as possible. Cut bureaucratic steps. Look to do functions in tandem rather than sequentially.

Yet balance speed with completeness.

Don't subject them to a generic solution within a few minutes, with the goal of adding the details later. This will give them a nega-tive first impression of your answering service, one from which you might never recover.

The goal is to minimize the time from when they hire you to when you're providing complete, first-class service. The longer you take, the more opportunity they have for buyer's remorse to set in. Take too long and they could cancel service before they even start.

Message Delivery: The TAS industry has made substantial progress with all the innovative options to get clients their messages and information quickly. Yet most of these capabilities exist on your platform, which means many other answering services have these options at their disposal too.

Look for other innovative ways to help your customers with their communication needs, delighting them in the process. This will be a key distinguishing characteristic to better serve them.

Billing: Have you ever received an invoice that was hard to understand? Did it contain descriptions that made little sense or line items that delineated confusing information?

Do the invoices your answering service sends carry these same issues? Information on most invoices reflects what the business needs to better manage the financial aspects of its operation. The side effect is a less-than-ideal presentation to customers.

This is backward. Don't frustrate customers with a confusing invoice just because it's what works best for you. Redo your invoicing with a customer-first mentality to better serve your clients.

Problem Resolution: Though you wish problems never arose with the service you provide to your clients, it happens. The obvious solution is to strive to minimize the occurrence of problems in the first place.

Yet when issues occur, how you react is critical. This includes how quickly you respond and how accurately you resolve the problem. A third, but often overlooked, element is how the customer reacts to your efforts. If you've corrected their concern but they don't realize it, you've still lost.

Moving Forward: As you review this list of areas for improvement, pick the one that offers the biggest potential impact to your clients. Then, work toward improving it. This will help you better serve your clients and stand out from your competition.

33

STREAMLINE SERVICE PROVISION

BE INTENTIONAL ABOUT WHAT YOU DO SO YOU CAN DO IT BETTER AND FASTER

R unning a telephone answering service is a labor-intensive endeavor. It takes staff to offer the personal service your clients expect. And staffing costs money, emerging as your greatest expense. It may be tempting to automate your service and thereby hold down costs, but don't do it.

Though automation may be a business strategy you elect to pursue, it removes you from the industry's core distinctive of having people help people.

Instead of seeking to streamline the service portion of your answering service, seek to streamline everything else. We'll expand on this in subsequent chapters. For now, we'll focus on doing the service portion of your TAS more effectively.

Here are some areas to consider:

Set Consistent Expectations: Consistency is the key to simplicity. Establish consistent expectations of what you want your staff to do and communicate them clearly. Repeat and reinforce as necessary. You never want your employees—especially your frontline ones—to be in a quandary of what to do or how they should react in a normal situation.

Shorten the Onboarding Process: You sold your client on

your service, so make sure they can use it without any unnecessary delay. Don't give time for buyer's remorse to set in. Get as close as you can to offering them instant gratification.

Setting up a new client requires many steps and involves multiple people, from programmers to training to accounting and possibly even the technology team. Remove as many steps and as many people as possible from the process. Set a goal to quicken the startup phase. Make it as short as possible without cutting too much.

Develop a Standard Operating Procedure: Establish a SOP for every recurring process. Have standards in place to support consistency.

Sometimes a SOP is a checklist to follow. Other times, it's the training process everyone receives. SOPs can also be rules to follow or policies to adhere to.

Variability is the enemy to providing streamlined service. Seek to remove every variable every chance you can by establishing SOPs. This lessens the chance for errors and problems.

Automate the Back End: While you should guard against the urge to save money by streamlining the provision of service through automation, automation has its rightful place behind the scenes. Automate as much of it as you can.

Seek to apply automation to your onboarding process, not only for clients but also for employees. Just as you want to serve your clients as quickly as possible, you want your staff engaged in productive work as fast as is reasonable. What can you do to automate their introduction to your company and optimize their training?

Also, seek to automate scheduling to the highest degree possible. Can you automate break schedules and lunches? What about QA (quality assurance) evaluations?

Simplify Rates and Billing: Look at your rate structure and your billing processes. For most services, this area has grown increasingly complex over time. What can you do to make it simpler? What packages can you merge or eliminate? Seek to have as few options as possible.

If you give a prospect ten rate plans to choose from, they'll have trouble deciding. If you give them only two, it's a much easier choice. Although two options are unlikely to fit every scenario, keep the number of plans as low as you can.

Likewise, seek to have as few billing elements as possible. Although the simplest rate structure is a fixed monthly fee and nothing more, that doesn't work for most services. After that, the next simplest is a base rate, included time or units, and the cost of overages. That's three elements. Resist the urge to add more. Don't have other charges or fees. This irritates clients and is a source of dissatisfaction, which leads to service cancellation.

Moving Forward: Follow these steps to improve the effectiveness of the service your TAS provides. This will reduce complexity and the associated errors that invariably result. It will also improve service and increase profits.

34

STREAMLINE AGENT HIRING

OPTIMIZE YOUR HIRING PROCESS TO REALIZE
FAST RESULTS

Have you ever offered a promising job candidate a position only for them to decline because they had already accepted a job with another company? I have. I took too long. Even though they claim to have preferred to work for me, they grabbed the first job offer that came their way.

People today—including job seekers—have little patience. Our world wants instant gratification and has little tolerance for waiting. Unless you want to continue losing qualified candidates, you need to optimize your hiring process. Look for ways to make it more efficient so you can hire the best applicants before someone else does.

Don't continue following yesterday's hiring practices, because they're no longer appropriate for today's workplace. What is the average time between a job seeker first expressing interest and you hiring them? I hope your answer isn't more than a week. Even a couple of days is too long. Can you get down to twenty-four hours? How about a same-day decision? Just how fast can you act?

Here is an idea to consider. Note that this isn't a proven plan to follow but merely a possibility to spark your creativity:

1. Online Self-Assessment: Once you've captured a prospective employee's attention, provide them with an online self-assessment tool that will allow them to determine if an answering service environment is a good fit for them. Present a series of questions that reflect work at your answering service. The more scenarios they align with, the better fit they are. Score their answers and immediately give them the results.

Then tell them: "People who score between X and Y tend to like working for our company, whereas people with lower scores may struggle to succeed in this position. Do you want to apply?"

This assessment occurs online, and automatically, with no involvement on your part.

Note that unless you take time to validate the outcome, don't record their score or ask them their results. To avoid a legal quagmire, let them use this tool anonymously to determine if they want to move forward.

2. Phone Screening Call: If they want to proceed after taking the online self-assessment, move them immediately to a prescreening evaluation over the phone. This is a standardized set of questions to rule out candidates who don't fit your criteria, such as people wanting full-time work when you're hiring part-timers or candidates seeking a business-hours position when your openings are for evenings and weekends.

You should script the call flow so that any of your agents can conduct the phone screen. Anyone who passes should move on to a phone interview.

3. Same-Day Phone Interview: For candidates who pass the phone screen, give them the option of an immediate phone interview, or let them schedule one. Yes, an immediate phone interview. Connect them to your hiring manager or HR department. Again, make this a structured process that provides an instant pass/fail outcome.

Though you may prefer an in-person interview, remember that all their work at your answering service will take place over the phone, so a phone interview should be more indicative of their capabilities than an in-person meeting.

4. Make an Immediate Offer: For candidates who pass the phone interview, make an offer at that point. Don't delay. Desiring to compare a group of candidates who pass the phone interview will not only take more time, but it also increases the risk of your best candidate receiving a job offer from someone else before you make yours.

Once you've made the offer, don't push them for an immediate yes/no answer. Though some people will accept right away, others will want to think about it. If that's the case, schedule a follow-up phone call.

Moving Forward: This idealized hiring process could take less than an hour. Though it will require effort to fine-tune each step and compress it into a sixty-minute procedure, you can do it.

Once hired, your next task is to optimize your onboarding and training process to make it just as efficient.

35

STREAMLINE AGENT TRAINING

LOOK TO IMPROVE NEW EMPLOYEE INSTRUCTION

N ow that you've hired an agent, the next step is their training. Seek to streamline it. There are two potential goals. One is to train better, and the other is to train faster. Ideally, you want to do both.

To address the speed element, look for ways to streamline training from both the company standpoint and the new-hire perspective. When you streamline the trainer component, you reduce training costs and decrease trainer hours. When you streamline the trainee component, the new employee becomes productive faster and does so at a lower cost. This reduces the chance of boredom or getting frustrated during training and quitting. It also allows them to generate revenue for your answering service faster.

Here are some techniques to streamline agent training:

One-to-Many Instruction: The more agents you can train at the same time by one instructor, the more efficient that trainer will be. This has the highest potential at larger answering services that hire and train more employees. Envision a classroom-style environment with one instructor training four, eight, or even twelve employees at a time.

But smaller operations that typically train one agent at a time can still look to employ one-to-many training opportunities. Even if one trainer instructs two trainees, it doubles the trainer's output.

Though some aspects of training may require one-on-one instruction, look to minimize those instances whenever possible. This allows you to maximize the instructor's effectiveness with one-to-many training scenarios.

Recorded Lessons: Look for segments of training that are highly repetitive. Video the instructor giving that lesson. Then, have future trainees watch the recording. This is a onetime investment that you can use repeatedly for many new employees for months or even years. Be sure to review the recording periodically to ensure the information hasn't changed. When a recording becomes out-of-date, make a new one.

Self-Study Opportunities: Not every part of agent training requires an instructor. New employees can conduct some aspects of the training by themselves. This may include reading training materials or engaging in hands-on interactive instruction. Though you might need to develop some of these tools yourself, you may be able to get others from your vendor or user group to work with you on developing these resources. Whenever possible, adapt what's already provided instead of making your own.

Fast Productivity: Does your answering service have a high-volume account or a group of accounts that are easy to serve? It might be worthwhile to structure training so that your new hires can handle just this one high-volume account or a group of straightforward accounts quickly. This will let them gain experience early in the training process, and it will allow them to be productive much faster.

After they've taken these specific types of calls for a while, they can return to training and prepare to handle your other accounts. Not only does this benefit your TAS by having these new hires generate billable transactions quickly, but it also benefits the employee by giving them a break in their training and letting them take calls—which is what you hired them to do.

Moving Forward: Streamline agent training to save money, improve results, and produce productive employees faster.

36

STREAMLINE CLIENT ONBOARDING

SPEED CAN BE A STRENGTH OR A WEAKNESS

How long does it take you to put a new client on service? How long should it take? I'm sure you can answer the first question quickly, but I imagine there might be a bit of angst in considering your response to the second one.

In a culture where people don't want to wait, there's a pressure to respond quickly when a business wants to use your answering service. But does that pressure to react fast push you to go too quickly?

Consider these scenarios.

Fast Activation: When you have a new client, everyone's excited. You're happy for more business, and they're eager to use your answering service right away. You assign their number, and they give you their information. So, let's go!

Many answering services strive to put new clients on fast. Sometimes they're even answering calls before all the information has been entered. In some cases, staff can answer a new client without first reviewing the information and not knowing the details they need to serve them well. Other times they can't. In the push for fast activations, attention to detail and quality may suffer.

Some answering services are too fast in adding new accounts. In their pursuit of speed, they sacrifice quality. Do you want your first impression with a new client to revolve around an error caused by going too fast?

Methodical Training: To counter the downsides of a fast-activation strategy, other answering services carefully program the account, review and test the information, and train staff. This can take days, even a week or more. Will the client tolerate waiting that long? Remember, they're impatient. They said *yes* to your sales offer, so in their minds they're ready to begin.

But you painted an impressive picture of the quality you provide, and they don't realize that good things take time.

Some services are too slow in putting on accounts. The result is a delay that fails to impress your client. Is that how you want to begin your business relationship?

Just Right: There's a middle point that balances speed with attention to detail. What is it? One hour? By the end of the day? Within twenty-four hours?

There's no right answer; you must determine the solution. Find a balance between going fast and being thorough, but don't accept the status quo. Continually ask, "How can we improve?"

Moving Forward: Seek ways to start new clients both faster and better. But never sacrifice one in pursuit of the other.

37

STREAMLINE BILLING AND COLLECTIONS

INCREASE CASH FLOW BY SHORTENING THE TIME BETWEEN BILLING CUTOFF AND PAYMENT RECEIPT

As you look at ways to be a responsive answering service, one critical, but too-often overlooked, area is billing and collections. This affects cash flow and is a critical consideration in maintaining the financial viability of your answering service. Each additional day you wait to receive payment is another day trying to operate without the money that's due you.

Let's look at some ways to streamline billing and collections.

Billing Cutoff Date: How close is your billing cutoff date to when you begin processing invoices? The goal is to make it as short as possible. If you bill monthly, what happens when the end of the month occurs on the weekend? What if it's a long weekend? Do you wait until Monday or the next business day to begin work on billing? If so, that's one, two, or even three extra days added to your collection cycle.

If you bill every twenty-eight days, you can strategically pick your billing cutoff date to be when you can best work on it, such as a Tuesday or Wednesday.

Billing Cutoff Time: When do you download or transfer your billing statistics? Though midnight is a logical cutoff time, does that make sense if you won't start processing information until 9 a.m.?

Though nine hours may not seem like much, it represents nine hours of billing that you can collect this billing cycle as opposed to the next one.

Regardless, the goal is to shorten the time between downloading your stats and sending invoices. Strive to make it the same day.

Sending Invoices: Most businesses today email their invoices. Do you? Mailing them adds an extra two or even three days to your collection cycle. Look for ways to get your invoices to your clients' payables department as quickly as possible. Is texting invoices an option? Many people open text messages within a few minutes. That's faster than email and much faster than snail mail.

Receiving Payments: Do you have clients mail you a check? That adds another couple of days to your collection cycle. Can you have them pay by credit card instead? Though credit card payments involve additional fees, it may be worth it to collect on time, especially for chronic late payers. What about ACH (Automated Clearing House) and EFT (Electronic Funds Transfer)? These are low-cost ways to collect faster.

Related to credit card and ACH payments is timing. When do you process those payments? Is it when you generate the invoice, at the due date, or in between? Shortening the number of days will allow you to collect faster and reduce your collection cycle. However, don't change your processing timing without first clearly communicating the new policy to your clients.

For further consideration, explore two related accounting principles: average collection period and accounts receivable turnover.

Moving Forward: Seek ways to shorten the time between your billing cutoff and receiving payment. This will improve your cash flow and increase the health of your answering service.

38

STREAMLINE ACCOUNTS PAYABLE

DISCOVER WHY YOU MAY NOT WANT TO FOLLOW CONVENTIONAL WISDOM FOR PAYABLES

T he standard business advice for accounts payable is to delay payment as long as possible, even beyond the stated due date—assuming you can get away with it. This benefits cash flow, providing more money available for day-to-day operations. This may be shrewd business, but it's not *good* business.

Although lengthening payables may make sense from a money standpoint, it may not be the best overall strategy. Here's why:

Build A Buffer: A business that mails payables at the 30-day mark or pushes payments beyond that, say perhaps to 45 days, has no cushion when cash flow gets tight and there's not enough money in their account to pay all the invoices that are one month old.

A business that pays invoices quickly, perhaps in one week, benefits by establishing a buffer for those times when it can't pay as quickly. After all, what vendor would care—or even notice—if they received your payment in ten days as opposed to the usual seven? Having a policy of paying invoices quickly builds a buffer for those times when remitting payment suffers a bit of a delay.

Act Ethically: Some businesses agree to their vendors' terms of service, such as net 30, knowing they have no intention of following through. Yes, they will pay, but it will happen when they want and not according to the agreement they committed to. This is not ethical. Stop doing it.

Reduce Needless Interruptions: When a business pays invoices late, even by a couple of days, it receives collection calls. Each call about a late or missed payment is an interruption to the person receiving the call. Now multiply this by every vendor you work with. That's a lot of employee time spent dealing with an avoidable problem, and it diverts them from work that's more important and more profitable.

Become a Preferred Customer: Whenever I have a special promotion to offer, who do I contact first? It's those who pay their bills quickly, followed by those who pay within 30 days. I never consider customers who pay late and cause me extra time chasing down the payments they committed to make. In short, becoming a preferred customer by paying invoices quickly has rewards, while those who pay late end up on a different list.

Consider your accounts payable policy and how that affects your vendors and your staff. Granted, you can't immediately go from paying in 30 days—or later—to paying the day the invoice arrives. But you can move in that direction.

First, take steps to pay all vendors within the timeframe they expect and that you agreed to.

Next, incrementally shorten your payables cycle one day at a time. Keep working on it until you can pay every invoice quickly. The ultimate accounts payable streamlining will occur when you can pay every invoice on the day it arrives. Your vendors will appreciate it, and your staff will respect you.

Moving Forward: Seek to be a company that always pays invoices on time and often faster—much faster.

39

STREAMLINE ADMINISTRATION

BE SURE TO ANALYZE YOUR OWN WORK FOR OPTIMIZATION OPPORTUNITIES

Now turn your attention to upper management: the admin function. Every role in every business carries a bit of fluff, some more than others. This includes upper management, also known as administration. Here are key areas to consider in streamlining your answering service's admin function:

What Can You Eliminate? What admin tasks fall short in producing a tangible benefit for your service? These include activities that once held value but no longer do, as well as work that never contributed to overall business success. Especially scrutinize projects that are done because they're enjoyable, and duties pursued because they seem essential. Analyze each one.

Ask yourself, what's the worst that could happen if no one did this chore? If the answer is nothing or if there's a risk of investing an inconsequential amount of time in the future, then cut that activity.

What Can You Streamline? Of the remaining tasks, consider how to make each of them more efficient. This includes removing steps that don't significantly contribute to the outcome, as well as cutting the number of people involved in the project. Each resource removed from the process makes it easier to do and less time-consuming. This frees up energy and staff for other activities of greater importance.

What Can You Delegate? For those items that pass the first screen—the ones considered essential to your service's profitability, viability, or effectiveness—and are streamlined, consider who should handle them. You may not be the right person for the job. Maybe you're overqualified to manage it, your time is too valuable to devote to it, or someone else is better suited to the task.

Look to delegate what you can. This will not only lighten your load, but it will also empower people on your team. Many want to take on more responsibility at your answering service. And if someone claims they're too busy to do your delegated assignment, challenge them to look at what existing tasks they can eliminate or delegate to others.

Act Now: Realizing the benefits of streamlining admin functions requires effort. If you think you're too busy to do this, you've just confirmed how essential this optimization project is.

Start by doing a time study of everything you do for at least a week. Yes, it's a hassle, but the information is invaluable. As a bonus, many people who keep a time log find it automatically makes them more efficient because they don't want to document their inefficiencies or poor time management.

Moving Forward: Once you determine how you spend your time, ask how important each task is to your answering service's overall well-being. Look to cut non-essential work. Streamline what remains. Delegate what you can.

40

STREAMLINE OTHER TAS PROCESSES

SEEK TO PROVIDE THE FAST RESPONSES YOUR
PROSPECTS AND CLIENTS EXPECT

W e live in an I-want-it-now culture, with people expecting quick responses to their inquiries. If they don't get what they want when they want it, they'll seek solutions elsewhere.

This is why you need to fine-tune your various answering service processes. The goal is to develop new ways of doing things so you can respond quicker to your present and future clients. We've already looked at ways to streamline your provision of service, agent hiring and training, client onboarding, billing, and administration, but there's more.

Here are some areas to consider.

Streamline Sales: As we asked earlier, how long does it take from the time a prospect clicks a button for more information until they're interacting with a person who can help them? An automated response that someone will get back to them doesn't count. Though this is a good practice, what matters to prospects is contact from a salesperson who can answer questions and move toward a successful close.

The patience of prospects is extremely short. The chances of success decrease noticeably as response times increase. For many situations, a five-minute response time is a new standard. Making prospects wait even thirty minutes dramatically decreases the chance of someone connecting with them and closing the account. That's why some companies push for a one-minute response time. Most prospects will wait sixty seconds before they contact another company.

This means you need to figure out a way that the information on the clicked form goes immediately to a salesperson who can contact them right away. Any other steps or delays are unacceptable.

Streamline Customer Service: Now you've turned a prospect into a client. Ideally, they'll have no customer service issues, but they probably will.

When responding fast to customer service inquiries, there are two considerations. The first is how quickly the client can share their concern with someone who can act upon it. The second is how quickly the customer service agent can implement and communicate the solution to the client. Address both issues, fine-tuning your processes to respond with speed and accuracy.

[Learn more in Peter's book, *Sticky Customer Service*.]

Streamline Technical Support: What about dealing with technical issues your clients encounter? Begin by looking at recurring problems that affect more than one client. What can you do to streamline them? You can develop a facts sheet to address each subject. You can email it to clients as an attachment or post it online and send them a link.

A second level is simplifying the process to resolve the technical concerns of one client. How can you respond faster and better?

Once you've fine-tuned the processes in all these areas, you can sit back and take it easy, right? Wrong! Don't accept the status quo, and don't assume that if something was good enough last year, it's good enough now.

Moving Forward: Always seek to do things faster and better. Other answering services are. If you want to keep up, so should you.

41

OPTIMIZATION PROCESS

HOW TO STREAMLINE YOUR ANSWERING SERVICE'S PROCEDURES

We've looked at several areas to streamline in your telephone answering service. In all cases, the goal was to achieve the same—or better—results more effectively. To realize this outcome, however, doesn't mean working harder. It means working smarter.

To optimize any of these processes—and others—look at the number of steps required, the time they take, and what can occur concurrently.

Reduce the Number of Steps: As time passes, any process becomes more complicated. The initial steps required remain, while new ones join them. As a result, most processes become bloated over time. Even though some of these steps are no longer required to achieve the desired outcome, or have a negligible impact on the result, your staff persists in doing them because they always have.

Scrutinize every process and ask if each step remains relevant. Too often, what was once important no longer is. Identify those tasks and cull them. For each step, consider the impact if you eliminate it. If it doesn't warrant its continued existence, cut it out and show your staff why it's no longer applicable. They may initially resist this change, but once they realize it will make their jobs easier, they'll quickly embrace the streamlined process.

Reduce the Time: Removing the number of steps required to complete a task should automatically make it faster. Now, look for other delays you can remove from the process. Does one person arbitrarily delay completing a task that's part of an overall process? Since they must do it anyway, why not do it right away?

Another opportunity to shorten how long a process takes is to look for areas you can automate. Why wait for a person to do something a computer can do automatically? Tap technology whenever possible.

Concurrent Paths: Next, realize that some things don't have to proceed linearly, with some tasks allowing for simultaneous execution. For example, when a client signs up for service, one person will need to program the account, while another person will set up billing. It may seem orderly to do one and then the other, but both actions can occur at the same time.

Like any business, an answering service thrives on processes. This ensures that work proceeds in a smooth and organized manner, producing the desired outcome. These processes, however, often swell over time, becoming inefficient and unwieldy.

Moving Forward: Look for ways to remove steps and shorten the time to complete them. This will result in achieving better outcomes and realizing the desired results faster.

WEBSITE

42

DOES YOUR ANSWERING SERVICE HAVE A GREAT WEBSITE?

REGARDLESS OF HOW YOU PROMOTE YOUR TAS, YOU NEED A WEBSITE

There are many ways to market your answering service, limited only by your creativity and budget. Regardless of which strategy you use, you need a website. Even if you claim you're not accepting new clients, you still need a website to help retain existing ones.

Let's make sure your website is a great one.

Your website stands as your make-or-break element to close sales. Regardless of your marketing tactics, prospects expect to find a website. Most times, your website will be part of your marketing campaign. But even if it isn't, buyers may still look for one. What they see will determine whether they say *yes* or *no*.

Impress them, and they're likely to sign up. Disappoint them, and they'll go to your competitor. And if you don't have a website, or they can't find it, you've lost their business.

What About Social Media? Some businesses, including those in the answering service industry, insist a website isn't necessary, that they get along just fine using social media. But using social media as your online home base is foolish. You don't own it and have no control over what happens there.

On social media, you're at the whim of corporate overlords. At any moment, your online social media presence could go away, or your audience's ability to see your content could face severe limitations. All social media platforms need to make money. At the most basic level, they want to charge you to reach your audience and show ads you can't control.

Though you might opt to get rid of social media altogether, you can alternately use it to point people to your website—your home base—which is the only online real estate you can own and control.

What About Print? In the old days, back before the internet, businesses relied on various forms of print media to promote themselves and gain new clients. This included the Yellow Pages, newspaper ads, and direct mail. When was the last time you saw the Yellow Pages? When was the last time you read a newspaper? And what do you do when you receive direct mail? You likely throw it away without opening it.

Even for specific print niches that still work, today's consumers expect you to have a website. Not to have one means you're not viable. You're invisible. At best, you're second rate.

What About Online Advertising? Many people love online advertising. It's easy to track and determine your ROI (return on investment). You can measure your success—or the lack thereof—fast. Though the call to action for online marketing can be to call a phone number, most involve a website. Even if the goal is to have the prospect pick up the phone, having a website adds essential credibility to your offer.

Rethink Your Website: View your website as your online home base. Use social media to point to it. Social media is ancillary to marketing, not central. And if you prefer print media, the results will be stronger if you have a great website riding shotgun. The same is true for online advertising. Without a website, you might get a lot of clicks but few conversions.

Scrutinize your website. Is it as good as it can be? Or does it look tired and dated? I've looked at a lot of TAS websites. Most could be better, and some are embarrassing. That needs to change.

Moving Forward: To successfully market your answering service, you need to have a great website. It's essential.

43

WHAT DOES YOUR WEBSITE DO FOR YOU?

MAKE THE MOST OF YOUR ONLINE PRESENCE TO BETTER SERVE CUSTOMERS AND GROW YOUR BUSINESS

Over the years, I've seen a wide range of TAS websites, from severely lacking to impressively professional. They fall into some common categories. Consider which category yours fits into. Then determine if it's the right one.

A Placeholder: Some websites are nothing more than placeholders. They may say "coming soon" or have generic text that gives no specific information. I suspect this is from companies that registered the domain names to use for email. Or maybe they are answering services that registered the names but never got around to setting up the sites.

Either way, be aware that prospects and others looking to learn about your business will stumble upon it. The message a placeholder website sends is not a good one. You'd be better off if it didn't exist.

An Online Brochure: Moving beyond a do-nothing placeholder website is turning it into an online brochure. Effectively, this means taking what once would have been in printed marketing materials and putting it online.

Typically, this begins as a one-page website. There's nothing wrong with this. At a basic level, an online brochure provides visitors with some information about your operation. It's a great start.

An Information Center: Building upon a website as an online brochure, add other content that prospects will find helpful. This means adding more pages. Besides your marketing information, you'll want a *homepage*, an *about* page, and a *contact* page.

You may also want a blog to post news and content marketing pieces, but don't jump into starting a blog without first thinking it through and making sure you or someone on your team has the commitment to produce regular content. (See chapter 26, "Consider Content Marketing.")

A Marketing Tool: You can expand your website beyond an information center and turn it into a marketing tool. You can add pages that cover services offered, specialties or industries served, testimonials or reviews, pricing, and a sign-up form.

Which ones you include will vary with your marketing strategy, so don't think you need to pursue every suggestion. Just add what makes sense for your situation.

A Client Support Resource: Until now we have covered website options from the perspective of a prospect. It should also have a section for clients. Provide client-specific information to help them get the most out of their experience with your answering service. You can also include a client portal to allow them to access messages, submit a customer service request, and update on-call or account information. You can also allow them to pay their bills online.

These options should require a customer login. This blocks prospects from accessing this information (or trolls intent on causing mischief).

Your Online Hub for All Interaction: The best websites are both a marketing tool and a client support resource. It becomes your online hub for communication with both prospects and clients.

If your website is currently at this level, well done. But that doesn't mean you're finished. Look for ways to make it simpler to navigate and more user-friendly.

Moving Forward: A website is never done and requires ongoing tweaking. The goal is that each change makes it better and more effective.

44

SEVEN TIPS TO IMPROVE YOUR TAS WEBSITE

DON'T JUST HAVE A WEBSITE; MAKE IT A GREAT ONE

Having a professional website is essential for any telephone answering service that wants to grow. The emphasis is on the word *professional*. Collectively, industry websites are much better than a decade ago, but too many TAS websites still aren't professional-looking or professional-sounding.

Here's how to develop a professional website for your answering service:

1. Clarify Your Brand: Before you do anything with your website, you need a clear, strong brand. This includes the overall image you want to project and the supporting materials, including logo, color palette, tagline, mission, and so forth.

2. Decide Who You Are: You must determine if you will brand yourself as a telephone answering service, a call center, a contact center, a BPO (business process outsourcer), or something else.

3. Establish Goals: What do you want your website to accomplish? It can be an online brochure to support your sales team, a means to capture leads, a way to order online, or an option to provide marketing collateral.

4. Hire an Experienced Website Developer: With your

brand, identity, and goals established, now hire a professional website designer. Though they could produce your logo, branding, and color palette, if you don't have all these other elements firmly in place before you call them, expect to pay more for them to help you work through these decisions— or you'll realize less-than-ideal results.

Also, ask them to use WordPress. Currently, over 40 percent of the websites worldwide use WordPress, and the number grows annually. It's open source, has a great online support community, and there are scads of developers to step in if your developer disappears, which can happen. As a bonus, it's easy enough to use that you can make most changes yourself.

5. Don't Survey Other TAS Sites: Avoid looking at other answering service websites for ideas. Instead, look at the successful websites of other professional service organizations. You don't want to look like other TAS websites; you want to look better. You should peer outside the industry to do so. Tell your designer which ones you like and why.

6. Hire a Writer: Your developer could write your content, or you could do it yourself, but the likely outcome is you'll end up sounding like everyone else. Instead, hire a professional freelance writer or journalist to interview you and write the content. Your website developer may have recommendations you can contact.

7. Refresh Every Couple of Years: In looking at TAS websites, I see a few that were great websites—ten years ago. Now they merely look dated and imply the same about the company. Plan to update yours about every two to three years. This shouldn't cost nearly as much as the initial site—unless you wait too long before doing the update.

Note that a refresh doesn't mean a complete overhaul. Sometimes switching to a new theme is all you need.

Moving Forward: Having a professional website is critical to helping your answering service grow. It's an important step toward a better tomorrow.

45

HOW TO MAKE YOUR WEBSITE SHINE

DEVELOP AN ESSENTIAL MARKETING RESOURCE

Having a great website to serve as your online home base is an essential element of your marketing plan.

Though you can hire a professional web developer to do this for you (as we covered in the prior chapter), you can also do it yourself. Either way, here are some tips to guide the process. Follow these and you'll be ahead of many industry websites.

Have a Clean, Fresh Design: To pursue a website that looks fresh and clean, avoid the opposite: a dated, cluttered website. Don't squeeze everything into a small area. Instead, use white space to make the content more inviting and readable. Stick with one common font and use black type on a white background. Anything else is hard to read, as well as trendy, which will become dated fast. Also, keep a simple color palette that matches your logo.

Prioritize Search Engine Optimization: I suspect you've heard of SEO (search engine optimization). If you're like most business owners, you're ignoring it or giving it scant attention. This is a mistake. The best-designed website will struggle without SEO, while a less than ideal one will get more traffic if it does a good job at optimizing content for search engines.

SEO is part science and part art. You need someone who can

master both. And just because they say they're an expert, doesn't mean they are. The proof is in the results. As an SEO guru optimizes your site, expect to see results within a month, two at the most. If your traffic isn't increasing, you've hired the wrong person.

How much should traffic increase under a good SEO program? The answer depends on how bad things are to start with, but the results must be measurable and should be significant.

SEO is an even more important issue in the age of AI. Without it, AI will ignore your site when answering questions or making recommendations. You want AI to know about your business; your website is how to make this happen.

Provide SEO Friendly Content: If you want people to find your site through organic search, make sure you have at least 300 words on every page. Search engines need to see that much to index it properly. This means not putting text in graphics, which search engines can't read. It also means avoiding making visitors click *more* to read additional information; be sure all the text on a page is readily available without an extra click.

Avoid Industry Jargon: Most answering service websites contain industry terms that most prospects won't understand—unless another answering service already trained them. Don't make a prospect speak your language to do business with you. Instead, speak their language. This means explaining your service in terms they can understand from a basic business perspective. Keep things simple, and you'll close more sales and do it faster.

Make It User-Friendly: If someone ever asks you how to navigate your website or where to find something, it's a clue that you need to simplify its structure. Ensure that it's user-friendly. Make it intuitive. Don't hide links to needed information. Visitors should be able to find everything from your homepage. The more clicks they need to make or the longer they need to search for something, the more likely they are to get frustrated and leave.

Focus on Mobile First: Most of your website visitors will use mobile devices. This means you need a mobile-first strategy for website design. Merely being mobile-ready isn't enough, though it's a good start.

View your website on a mobile device and see how easy or hard it is to navigate. I've been to some websites on my smartphone and was so frustrated that I gave up and went to my computer. Few prospects, however, will bother to do that.

Proof Content and Test Links: I'm surprised at how often I see navigation errors and typos on websites. Website designers are weak in these areas, so you need to check. Get as many people reviewing your website as possible. Even more valuable is asking people who don't use answering services to give you feedback.

Moving Forward: Apply these tips when you update or overhaul your website. You'll get increased traffic, fewer complaints, and more sales.

46

THE ESSENTIAL PAGES EVERY TAS WEBSITE SHOULD HAVE

AN EFFECTIVE WEBSITE DOESN'T NEED TO BE BIG, BUT IT MUST COVER THE BASICS

Though some services can fix their failing websites by updating them, other sites need a complete overhaul.

Regardless of the situation, every website should have five essential pages.

1. Homepage: Your homepage should embrace visitors and draw them in. It should give them a reason to stick around and explore the content on your site.

Don't make your homepage about you. Focus on your audience; make it about them. This is hard to do well. To see if your words resonate with your audience, ask someone who doesn't know you or your business to read your homepage and tell you what they think. Adjust the text as appropriate to hone your message to resonate with visitors, that is, your prospects.

2. Services: Next, you need a page that lists your services. Don't provide too many options, or you will overwhelm them. Ideally, give them two options. That makes it easiest for them to decide. The more options, the harder you make it for them to choose. If it's too complicated, they'll go elsewhere.

Only listing two service options, however, presents a challenge. Three would be okay, four at the most.

Don't list every option you offer on this page. Instead, include the popular ones you want to sell. Then add something about contacting you for custom solutions. Most times, you should include pricing. The only exception might be if you are a premium provider and don't want to cover pricing until after you've sold them emotionally on the value of your service. (See chapter 30, "How to Handle Pricing on Your Website.")

3. Get Started: The next page should explain how easy it is for a prospect to become a client. Businesses that have used answering services will know what to expect and will skip this page, so write the content for someone who has never used an answering service. Spell things out for them in an easy-to-follow list.

They may not be familiar with call forwarding, for example. Explain it. They won't know which billing package they should select. Give them guidelines to figure it out. The goal is to make hiring you simple, easy-to-understand, and painless.

End this page with the call to action, designed to move them from prospect toward becoming a new client. This may include an information form to get more information or a phone number to call.

4. About Us: After these pages, include a section that talks about your answering service. The goal is to make your service shine while hinting at how its unique characteristics will benefit your prospects. Talk about anything that will make your answering service stand out. This could include how long you've been in business, awards you've won, and your industry leadership or community involvement.

Every answering service talks about its great staff, so should you. Share your vision to serve your clients. Talk about your quality service, easy-to-understand invoices, and the outcomes your clients can expect.

Don't be afraid of making this page too long, but make sure it's easy for visitors to scan. If they're interested, they'll read whatever you put there. At the end, you can list all of your client testimonials, though you may also want to sprinkle selected testimonials throughout the other pages of your site.

5. Contact Us: The final page should tell prospects how to reach you. At a minimum, there should be a phone number, but most people expect an email address as well. Many people will expect and use a contact form.

Consider listing your social media pages. This, however, assumes they're up to date and you're active on them.

Unless you're trying to obscure where you're located, include your mailing address. If you have multiple offices, this is a great place to list them.

Though your essential contact information should prominently appear on every page, include all options here. Some prospects will immediately look for a *contact us* page.

Bonus Considerations

Here are some other items to consider for your website.

Client Portal: Assuming you have a client portal, add a login link for your clients.

Employment: If you're like most services, you're looking for quality staff. Include an employment link. On this page, sell them on the desirability of working for your answering service, and make it easy for them to apply. (See chapter 34, "Streamline Agent Hiring.")

Note that *client portal* and *employment* aren't part of the five essential items and don't warrant a main menu tab, but they should be someplace. One option is in a header that appears at the top of every page.

Blog: Some answering services have a blog, which they use to post content marketing pieces. (See chapter 26, "Consider Content Marketing.") This is an option you should take only if you're committed to posting regular, valuable content. For most answering services, a blog is a time-consuming item that's not worth the effort.

A blog, however, is a great long-term move that will engage your audience, improve your SEO rankings, and help you stand out in the industry. (Unlike *client portal* and *employment*, list your blog on one of your main navigation tabs.)

Moving Forward: When you improve or overhaul your website, you'll attract more visitors. It will help turn prospects into clients. You'll sign them up faster and keep them longer.

47

DISCOVER THE KEYS TO SEARCH ENGINE OPTIMIZATION

YOUR WEBSITE ISN'T FINISHED UNTIL IT'S OPTIMIZED FOR SEARCH ENGINES

You have a website for your telephone answering service. That's the first step in establishing your online presence. But is your website doing all that you want it to? Does it meet your expectations?

If you're not enjoying the traffic you want to have, the answer may be search engine optimization (SEO). As the name suggests, SEO makes your website more attractive to search engines. If you impress them, they'll show your content to more people searching for answering service solutions or the expert content you've posted.

Your website designer should have handled SEO for your pages when they designed your site, but not all do, or they may do so haphazardly. Ask if they did. Then verify. You may need to add SEO information yourself or tweak what is already there. Regardless, the content you later add will need search optimization too.

Here are the keys to successful SEO.

Content Is Key: Good SEO starts with great content. But don't produce content for search engines. Instead, write for people. Put visitors first and search engines second.

If you pursue the opposite strategy and produce content with an

SEO-first mentality, you may see a bump in traffic, but visitors will quickly bounce once they discover your content is awkward to read or not what they expected. It's a prime example of the adage of winning the battle but losing the war.

Avoid Shortcuts: Successful SEO is an investment in the future. Adapt a long-term perspective when optimizing your website for search engines, and you'll enjoy lasting results with traffic that matters.

Yes, there are ways to game the system and garner a short-term spike in traffic. But it isn't sustainable. And most of these get-traffic-quick schemes hurt your site in the long term and end up working against you. These are called black-hat strategies. Basically, it's cheating.

Though nefarious SEO practitioners will continue to develop new ways to avoid doing the hard work of search engine optimization, the search engine companies strive just as hard to negate these cheats.

This means that to stay ahead, you'll continue to need to find new strategies to trick search engines. Don't go this route. Instead, take the high road. When you do, you'll enjoy better long-term results.

Outsource with Care: Though you can learn SEO and successfully implement it (more on SEO in the next chapter), many companies opt to outsource it instead. It seems too daunting, the learning curve is too steep, or they lack the time. So they seek SEO professionals to do the work for them.

Unfortunately, it's hard to assess the abilities and effectiveness of individuals and companies that offer SEO services. Most talk a good game, but not all can produce. Too many will only perform basic steps you can easily do yourself.

Sometimes they haven't kept up with the industry and recommend techniques that once worked but no longer do. Other times they unknowingly—or knowingly—use black-hat tactics that cause problems in the end and damage your website's search engine reputation.

There's no effective way to vet an SEO professional, but referrals from happy, long-term clients are key. You should expect measurable results. If an SEO vendor can't provide that, then they don't deserve your business.

This isn't to disparage all SEO providers. There are good ones out there who are worth every dollar they charge. The challenge is finding them and making sure they'll benefit your TAS.

Addressing these SEO elements will help search engines find, appreciate, and promote your site and its content.

Moving Forward: For SEO success, make visitor-focused content, avoid damaging shortcuts, and select your SEO vendor with care—or do it yourself.

48

DIY SEARCH ENGINE OPTIMIZATION
CONSIDER HANDLING SEO IN-HOUSE

To keep SEO in-house, use the Yoast SEO plugin. It has a great tutorial built into it. Read and do what it says. This will put you ahead of most other sites.

Here are some key points to get you started, but don't stress out if this seems overwhelming. Take them one step at a time.

Title: Every page or post will have a title for visitors. Write a title that will capture their attention. Beyond this, there's also an SEO title working behind the scenes. This is for search engines. Search engines will evaluate the title and display it in their search results.

Description: Next is a page or post description, called a meta description. Your visitors won't see this directly, but it displays in search results. You want this meta description to provide information that will grab reader attention and please search engines at the same time.

Keywords: This isn't one word but a phrase. The content on each page or post should revolve around this keyword phrase. Avoid repeating keyword phrases on different pages and posts. Make sure the content includes your keyword phrase multiple times without overusing it.

Headings: A well-written page or post will use subheadings every couple hundred words. Search engines like this, and it helps because most people scan content. Make your headings bold and add heading tags, such as H2 or H3. (Use an H1 tag only once, for the title of your page or post.)

Images: Every page or post should have an engaging graphic or photo that relates to the content. Give the image a name that reflects it, such as "professional phone answering." Don't use "image1" or "Dx23ga234k." Then, add relevant SEO alt text to the image. (We'll cover more about images in the next chapter.)

Link Strategy: It's a good practice to link every page and post to another one. Also, add one outbound link per post to a high-authority site, that is, one that gets a lot of traffic.

Content Length: Have a minimum of three hundred words but aim for at least five hundred. Anything shorter than three hundred doesn't give search engines enough content to analyze, so they may skip that page or make a wrong determination.

Web Address: A final consideration that's easy to cover is the words in the web address (also called a URL or Uniform Resource Locator) for that page or post. Make sure they reflect the theme of the content and include its keyword phrase.

Moving Forward: For DYI SEO success, put visitor-focused content first, avoid damaging shortcuts, and intentionally work to improve each page and post.

The worst thing you can do is nothing. That's the most ineffective SEO strategy of all.

49

HOW TO HAVE A FASTER TAS WEBSITE

SPEED AND RESPONSIVENESS MATTER FOR YOUR ONLINE PRESENCE

Having a website for your telephone answering service is the first step in creating your online presence. Then you need to keep it up to date and add content to stay relevant. But there's a third element, one which many businesses overlook. It's website speed. Do your pages take too long to load? Is your site sluggish?

Know that in today's I-want-it-now world, impatient people won't wait for a slow site to display its content. They'll bounce to your competitor. Each tenth of a second of delay increases the likelihood of someone leaving your site in frustration.

Yet this is a problem you can solve. Here are some items to consider.

Hosting: The biggest factor influencing a website's speed is the hosting. Shared hosting is the cheapest option but the slowest. This is because hundreds, likely thousands, of websites all run through one server. If any one of them has problems or encounters traffic spikes, every site on that server will suffer.

The key is to move away from shared hosting. Making this change is the quickest way to increase the speed of your website. Though there are many options once you move past shared hosting, all of them will provide a faster, more responsive website. And all of them will cost more.

Though you'll pay more for faster website hosting, this is not a place to skimp.

Graphics: The images on your website also affect its speed. A site with no pictures will be faster than one with images, but today's users expect visuals on a website. A straight-text site will be off-putting and look dated.

The first consideration is image format. Though PNG files have a higher quality, JPG files are perfect for online, and they're also much smaller. Though exceptions exist, converting PNG files to JPG most always results in a much smaller file size, which loads faster.

Consider the dimensions of your image. Though websites resize large graphics to fit smaller spaces, the better solution is to upload the right-sized image to begin with. Don't weigh your site down with large images that will never display at full size.

Bloated Features: Are you bogging down your website with features you don't use or need? For WordPress, which accounts for over 40 percent of all websites, these extra options are called plugins and widgets. Other platforms use names such as apps, extensions, or add-ons.

Only install the features you need and delete everything you don't use. Consider the utility of each feature. Does it truly add value to your site, or does it just seem cool?

The fewer things running in the background of your website, the faster it will load and the fewer problems you will encounter. It's an ideal example of the saying that *less is more*.

Moving Forward: Don't accept a slow website. It will cause you to lose business and frustrate users. Instead, take steps to make your website faster. This will cost some money and take time, but it's an investment worth making.

MINDSET

50

ANSWERING SERVICE FUNDAMENTALS

THREE FOUNDATIONAL WORDS DESCRIBE A TELEPHONE ANSWERING SERVICE

Take a moment to consider the foundational underpinnings of your answering service operation. Three words are both fundamental and insightful:

Virtual: An answering service provides a virtual service. It's been that way from the very beginning, over a century ago.

From your clients' perspectives, the TAS industry has never done work on-site, but remotely. Your staff's presence is not tangible, but virtual. As the previous century ended, some answering services began promoting the concept of the virtual receptionist.

This was nothing new, but as a concept, it was. Today, many entrepreneurs and small businesses tap into the parallel concept of a virtual assistant. This is a money-saving means to accomplish routine tasks with speed and precision. Answering services need to capitalize on this trend by touting their specialized version of a virtual assistant.

An answering service is virtual.

Scalable: Often technology carries the label of scalable. This means its scope can easily increase or decrease to meet changing user needs. Although answering services often have scalable technology, they remain labor intensive. Labor is not scalable.

From the perspective of your clients, however, you offer a scalable service. If you normally take one call at a time for a client and two come in at once, you *scale up* to handle the extra work. Then you *scale down*.

What happens if they close early, their receptionist is sick or on vacation, or they want everyone at a staff meeting? You automatically scale up to take their extra calls. Conversely, if they decide to extend their hours and stay open until seven instead of closing at five, you scale down accordingly to meet their new expectations.

They can't scale like that in their office. An answering service can.

Outsource: Though outsourcing—especially as it relates to phone calls—had its reputation tarnished by offshore outsourcing done poorly, the reality remains that outsourcing shines as a key business strategy. Outsourcing work provides flexibility and controls costs.

Businesses wishing to run a lean, effective operation know that outsourcing is a smart way to do this. Another significant reason to outsource is that many businesses are reluctant to hire staff. They cite overhead costs—especially healthcare expenses—and the legal hurdles to un-hire staff when no longer needed.

As a prudent alternative, they outsource whatever they can, whenever they can. As such, an answering service is an invaluable outsource provider.

Moving Forward: As you view your TAS, embrace the reality that you are a virtual, scalable, outsource provider. Use this to guide your strategy and promotion.

51

ANSWERING SERVICES HELP PEOPLE COMMUNICATE

SHIFT YOUR MINDSET FROM THE PAST TO EMBRACE THE FUTURE

I n recent years, it seems everything has changed—even more rapidly and profoundly than usual. Your response has been as always: adapt, adjust, and accelerate toward a new tomorrow.

To do this, you re-examined your staffing, from hiring to training, from scheduling to supervising. You may have sent people home to work, whether for the short-term or permanently. You fine-tuned your sales and marketing efforts to redefine success in an environment where the rules have changed. Coupled with this is the morphing of how you manage your answering service and staff in a way that's consistent with these changes.

It's also an appropriate time to revisit the *why* of telephone answering services.

It's easy to think of yourself as being in business to answer telephone calls for your clients. Though true, it's also a limited perspective. A more insightful view is to think of yourself as being in business to help people communicate. This may use the telephone, or it may tap into other communication channels. Don't lose sight of this.

People today communicate through email, text messaging, and social media. They also increasingly visit websites to solve problems, place orders, and connect securely. None of these involve the telephone, which is the predominant channel in the TAS industry and much of what you do. Yet you may not want to ignore these other channels either.

When you reimagine yourself as facilitating communication instead of only answering calls, you open a door to new possibilities. You then become a telephone answering service that processes emails, handles text messaging, and monitors social media for clients. You connect to their websites for text chat and assisted browsing opportunities. And yes, you also answer the telephone.

We'll expand on this in the next chapter when we talk about diversification.

Moving Forward: Shift your mindset from what was to embrace what is and what will be.

52

DON'T PUT ALL YOUR EGGS IN ONE BASKET

ANSWERING SERVICES SHOULD SEEK TO DIVERSIFY THEIR SERVICE OFFERINGS

D iversification is a wise business move to make your TAS more resilient to changing market conditions and external threats.

One diversification option is to become a multichannel provider. A wise approach that aligns with the core mission of facilitating client communications is to handle additional channels. This can include email processing, text services, web-based chat interaction, and social media monitoring.

Some answering services have moved in this direction with varying degrees of success. Others have contemplated it but have yet to act.

Another camp is those who have resisted offering other communication channels. I get that. Pursuing what is different presents challenges and is scary. Yet it's important for any business—including an answering service—to diversify its service offerings to better prepare for the future.

Whatever your perspective of this multichannel strategy, here are some ideas to help you move forward and realize success.

Select One Channel: Don't pursue a multichannel strategy by diving into every opportunity at once. Strategically select one option and resist the urge—no matter how tempting—to let another channel distract your attention.

Which channel are you most comfortable pursuing? Though this is a good place to start your deliberation, don't stop at this point. Next, evaluate the strength of your existing staff. Which channel best connects with their inherent skill set? Third, check with your vendor to see which option they can best and most easily provide through your current system. You'll want to integrate this new channel with your existing answering service platform. The last step, which could also be your first one, is to survey your existing client base and gauge their interest for each channel option.

Ideally, select the channel your existing staff has the skills to address, works on your current platform, and interests your established client base.

Proceed with Care: Once you've selected a second communication channel to pursue, plan carefully before you proceed. Don't announce this new service and solicit customers expecting to figure it out as you go. Train your staff. Test your platform. Anticipate potential problems and adjust as needed. Do all this before you sign your first client to this new channel.

Market the Channel: Once you've done all the needed preparation, now is the time to promote this new service. Start with your existing client base. You could even handpick clients predisposed to work with you and help you fine-tune your offering.

After you've added the service to all your existing clients who are interested in it, begin a sales and marketing campaign to solicit new business specifically for this channel. As a bonus, you can cross-sell them on your voice channel.

Master This Channel: As you gain success in the second channel, resist the urge to add another one too quickly. Excel with this channel before you diversify further into a third one. Don't rush, but don't coast either.

Repeat When Ready: Once you've achieved operational and financial success on your second channel, you're ready to replicate the process with a third. You may desire to expand quickly and repeat your success. But it may also be wise to take a strategic pause to settle into a new rhythm of offering two channels before you add a third. Just be sure not to remain there too long.

Moving Forward: Diversify your service offerings to become a multichannel provider. Your future will thank you.

53

CENTRALIZED OR NOT

CONSIDER WHETHER DECENTRALIZATION IS
IN YOUR BEST INTEREST

B y classification, a telephone answering service is a call
center: a centralized place where calls are made and
received. Yet many of today's answering services are
neither. They are not centralized, nor do they deal only with calls.
The label *contact center* more accurately reflects the current reality of
many operations: handling various forms of contact, including
phone calls.

This, however, doesn't address the reality that answering services
are increasingly not centralized, but dispersed, with multiple locations and even home-based agents.

Centralization Benefits: A centralized telephone answering
service is easier to manage and operate. It's the foundational
mooring of the past.

Decentralization Benefits: Given the benefits of centralization, decentralization carries a fresh set of benefits.

A key reason to decentralize is to tap new labor markets. After
all, it's hard to grow your TAS when you lack qualified workers.
Opening a second location near where workers live makes sense.

A second reason is redundancy. With two locations, each one

can back up the other. If both are fully self-contained and interconnected, they represent an elegant disaster recovery plan.

A third benefit is time-zone shifting. Imagine one location's midafternoon lull meshing with another location's 5 p.m. rush. Or what about a location in another part of the world whose first-shift staff answers third-shift calls for the United States?

Last, consider a completely decentralized answering service with every agent working from home. This broadens the labor pool even more, provides the greatest flexibility, and can reduce or even eliminate real estate costs.

Moving Forward: A decentralized answering service isn't for everyone, but it offers intriguing possibilities.

54

WHY DO SOME ANSWERING SERVICES GROW WHILE OTHERS STRUGGLE?

FIVE KEY CONTRIBUTORS TO ANSWERING SERVICE SUCCESS

O ver the years, some answering services get larger, while others don't. Though it may be because of bad timing or being in the wrong place, let's consider some characteristics that can contribute to answering service success.

This isn't a scientific analysis or a guaranteed checklist. Instead, it's a list of key characteristics that will help tip the balance in favor of growth, profits, and quality.

1. Strong Leadership and Management: Does an answering service need a leader or a manager? It requires both. A leader plans for tomorrow, while a manager handles today. Having one without the other leads to an imbalance in the operation and promotes frustration among staff and clients.

Though one person can be both a leader and a manager, sometimes it's wise for one person to lead and a second person to manage.

2. A Capable Management Team: When an answering service starts from nothing, the owner needs to wear many hats. For existing answering services, however, having one person attempt to handle everything is a bad idea, as something critical gets missed.

That's why it takes a team to run a TAS. As the service grows, the number of people on the team grows with it.

Two common mistakes answering services make are growing a team too slowly and growing it too fast. Successful growth requires a thoughtful balance.

3. No Weak Links: It takes several departments for a successful answering service. Operations is the biggest. Also needed are sales and marketing, accounting, and technical. A capable administrative team holds everything together, as guided by an effective leader. Each of these units must pursue excellence in all it does. There can be no weak links, or the answering service will struggle.

For example, if operations produces high-quality work but sales doesn't add enough new accounts, it doesn't matter how good the quality is because there won't be enough accounts to serve. Conversely, if sales and marketing adds new clients fast, but poor quality and customer service drives them away faster, it's a losing situation.

4. Attention to Detail: Details matter. It matters whether you're taking a message, programming equipment, setting up a client, sending an invoice, or leading a team. Doing 90 percent of the job isn't good enough. It requires 100 percent to achieve success.

5. Industry Involvement and Networking: Too many answering services function in isolation. They don't attend industry events, network with other answering services, or work to make the industry better. They toil in isolation, hoping they can figure everything out on their own.

Even if this works, it won't work as well as if they had regular input from others in the industry to encourage them with new ideas and provide motivation. Though some answering service leaders may claim they don't have the time or the money to get involved, the truth is they can't afford not to.

Look at your answering service operation through the lens of these suggestions. Then, determine what area needs attention and seek to improve it. As you do, you could very well end up realizing the outcomes you seek.

Moving Forward: Following these five tips may not guarantee answering service growth and success, but they will certainly place the operation in a better position than without them.

55

THE POWER OF NO

LEARNING TO SAY NO OPENS THE DOOR TO YES

I n your TAS, you're beset with continuous interruptions that demand your attention. You want to keep the staff happy and retain clients. This means you must put out the day-to-day fires, but that too often results in neglecting the long-term, year-over-year needs of your business.

You need to say *no* more often. Then you'll have room to say *yes*. Here are some areas to say *yes* to.

Maximize Profit: Regardless of why you're in the answering service industry, you must earn a profit to stay in business. (Even a nonprofit needs to have a positive cashflow.)

There are two ways to increase profit. One is to reduce costs, and the other is to increase revenue. Though you can increase revenue by selling more, the better way is to make sure each client is profitable. Analyze profitability every month and work to make unprofitable accounts profitable.

Improve Quality: As a service business, quality is essential. If quality is poor—or even average—it's harder to keep clients and land new ones. This makes it difficult to turn a profit, as well as develop staff and grow the business.

It's hard to say whether you should pursue quality first and then profit or profit and then quality. They're interdependent.

Develop Staff: Having a reliable team to run your business and optimize it is key. Too often, you hope a great team will just happen, but that seldom occurs. Most of the time, you need to groom staff, preparing them for the roles you envision. Therefore, be intentional in employee development.

Grow Your Business: A benefit of the telephone answering service industry is monthly recurring revenue. No client, however, stays with you forever. Clients eventually cancel. This happens every month. That means replacing departing clients with new ones, which falls to sales and marketing.

At a minimum, you need to keep even. Ideally, your service should grow. A shrinking client base is a symptom of a greater problem, one that should have been addressed earlier.

Moving Forward: Saying *no* to things that aren't critical provides the space and time to say *yes* to those things that are. Pick the essential items your answering service needs most to survive and say *yes* to them before agreeing to any other opportunities.

56

IS THE TAS MARKET REALLY
SHRINKING?

CONSIDER THE INDUSTRY-WIDE SITUATION

I t doesn't require much of a look at the telephone answering
service industry to know that the number of answering
services has been dramatically decreasing in recent decades.
Though we don't have exact numbers, most everyone agrees there
are fewer players in the industry today than at any time in recent
memory.

But this isn't because the industry is in trouble. In fact, it's just
the opposite. Many businesspeople and entrepreneurs see an opportunity to grow and make money. They are bullish about the industry.
They believe in the idea of helping businesses by serving people
over the phone.

These folks have been on a buying spree. Industry consolidation
runs rampant. While this consolidation provides serious challenges
for vendors and associations, it does not spell doom for the industry
overall.

Another thing that's a struggle to verify is market size. Although
the number of actual answering services is on the decline, the
number of TAS customers may not be. Even more, the amount of
revenue generated industrywide may be on the upswing.

Moving Forward: The TAS market isn't shrinking as much as it's changing. Be sure to change with it.

57

SEIZE THE PRESENT

EMBRACE TODAY AS AN OPPORTUNITY TO FORM A BETTER TOMORROW

Now is the time to move toward an improved future. It starts with embracing the opportunities you have in front of you at this moment.

What might those be?

It might involve personnel, such as a new hire, a restructuring, or fixing a broken team.

Could it be technology? To implement or fully master what's already installed, to buy something new, or to replace something that's inadequate.

What about operations? You could seek to streamline an outdated process, establish a procedure, or simplify the complicated.

Then there's sales and marketing to tackle: master online ads, overhaul sales collateral, or update an ineffective website.

There's plenty to do, and each thing you do will help pave the way for a better tomorrow.

Today Is the Day: Today is the day to step into your future. Don't delay. Don't wait until tomorrow.

You shouldn't delude yourself into thinking that next week will be a better time to embark on an essential project. Promising yourself that you'll make a fresh go of it tomorrow merely serves to delay forward progress.

Putting things off until tomorrow can easily become next week and then next month. Before you know it, it's a new season, and then the year is over. Don't wait for a better time to launch important initiatives.

Start today.

Focus on One Thing: You likely have more great ideas than you'll ever have time to do. If you try to do them all, you'll end up finishing none. Therefore, pick one thing that will make tomorrow better. Then do it. You won't wrap up this project in one day, but the work you do today will bring you one day closer to completing it.

Then Move to the Next Task: Once you complete one item, it's time to start the next. Though taking a day off to catch your breath is enticing, it also threatens to negate the habit you just formed of using today to produce a better tomorrow.

Moving Forward: Make today the day you take an intentional step toward your future.

STRATEGIC
CONSIDERATIONS

58

CONDUCT A YEAR-END REVIEW

TO KNOW WHERE YOU'RE HEADED YOU MUST FIRST DETERMINE WHERE YOU ARE

Year-end is an especially busy time at many answering services, but this isn't an excuse to focus on the present and stop thinking about the future. In fact, December is an ideal time to give some thought to where you are and to what lies ahead so you can prepare for next year.

If you don't know where you are, it's impossible to get to where you want to be. Take time to evaluate your current situation. This will form the basis for moving forward with intentionality. Here are some things to assess:

Staff: Let's start with the backbone of your answering service, your employees. They make you shine, but they can also produce problems, affecting your clients, the schedule, and profitability. In short, they can make or break your business.

Here are some questions to ask:

- **Telephone Staff**: Do you have enough frontline employees to answer calls? Don't worry (too much) if your answer is no; you're in good company. This provides you with an opportunity for improvement.

- **Staffing Model**: Do you have a centralized workforce, a distributed one, or a hybrid plan? What elements of this work for you? Which ones do not? What needs to change?
- **Turnover Rate**: Do you struggle to achieve an acceptable turnover rate? Regardless of where you're at now, what steps can you take to lower it?
- **Agent Quality**: Are you producing the quality service you aspire to offer and that your clients expect? Can you quantify your answer, or is it wishful thinking?
- **Non-Operations Staff**: Do you have adequate management and support personnel? Besides operations, look at accounting, sales, marketing, and technical roles, as well as administration. Consider your strongest areas and your weakest. How can you keep top employees? How can you best help those who struggle?
- **Yourself**: Do you have adequate time to address what's most essential for your answering service's long-term viability? Or do you spend too much time handling day-to-day minutiae? What steps can you take to be the leader your answering service needs?

Vendors: Your platform provider is a critical element of your operation's success. Leading vendors strive to enhance their offerings every year, providing new capabilities and opportunities to add value.

Look at your annual expenses to use their products. This includes onetime charges, subscriptions or leases, and other ongoing costs. Is the vendor easy to work with? Do they provide you with what you need to achieve your goals? How is their tech support?

And if your vendor isn't providing what you need or keeping pace with the industry, consider what you can do to help them achieve the results you want. Work with them, not against them. Changing vendors is the last thing anyone wants to do, so your first goal should be to make the best of what you have.

Industry Developments: Here are some common answering service industry trends to consider:

- **Consolidation**: The industry continues to consolidate. This produces an opportunity to sell. It also provides niche markets for nimble players to capture.
- **Competition**: At the same time, the remaining operations encounter increased competition in a national and even international marketplace. How can you make your service stand out?
- **Labor Market**: Most services struggle more than ever to find, hire, and keep qualified employees. Successfully addressing this dilemma could provide the biggest boost to your operation.
- **Technology**: The next consideration is technology, which allows you to do more and do so with greater ease, but it comes at the cost of an increased investment, coupled with increased configuration complexities.

What else would you add to this list?

Marketplace Opportunities: You compete in a national market, but you exist in a local one. What can you do to distinguish yourself in your community? What can you do to rise above other providers around the country?

Financial Situation: Look at the money side of your answering service. Two common items to address are increasing the money coming in and decreasing the money going out. Other items are access to capital and building up a reserve fund.

Moving Forward: Don't try to tackle this lengthy list all at once. Work on it over time, adding to it and fine-tuning it as you go. As you move toward the completion of this effort, a strategy to move forward will emerge.

59

DO YOU HAVE A PLAN?

IF YOU PURSUE NOTHING, THAT'S WHAT YOU'LL ACHIEVE

I'm a big advocate of planning. This means that I have a plan for each day and a plan for the week. I have a plan for the month and for each quarter. I also have a plan for the year. It's not elaborate, but it is written. It guides me in all I do.

Do you have a plan for this year? If not, no worries. Start one today. If you follow it with care, you'll finish the year strong.

Here are some ideas to consider:

Grow Your TAS: Most answering services want to get bigger. No one wants to command a sinking ship. And few people enjoy working for a business that's drifting along. Everyone wants to see sales and revenue trend upward.

Your growth goal can be a percentage or a net number of new clients. You can make it aggressive or stay conservative. The main thing is to pursue an increase in size. This will help you achieve greater economies of scale and improve revenue potential.

Pursue Opportunities: Opportunities surround every answering service. The problem is seizing them. Too often in the TAS industry, the attention becomes dealing with the day-to-day, leaving no time for tomorrow, let alone the rest of the year.

These opportunities could include pursuing a new market,

acquiring another service, or investing in technology. It might be time to reorganize your business, streamline operations, or overhaul sales and marketing.

Resolve Problems: Just as there are opportunities all around us, there are also problems. (I strive to view problems as opportunities in disguise.) Problems seldom go away on their own. Instead, they fester, getting bigger and worse with time. Pick the largest problem facing your TAS and make it your goal to minimize or eliminate that problem this year.

Hire Key Staff: Most answering services persist in a constant state of hiring. Because of the need to keep a full schedule of trained agents, it's hard to divert attention to mid- and upper-level management concerns. But you must. Should you add a position? Do you need to groom a replacement for one person so you can promote them? Is there some work you should offload to give you more time to lead, strategize, and succeed?

You can't tackle all these items at once; that would be impossible. You can, however, pursue one or maybe two. But if you don't make it part of your annual plan, it's likely you'll never get around to it.

Moving Forward: As you plan for the year, don't get carried away. Keep it simple. Make it attainable. Then, by year's end, you can take inventory and celebrate the great things you accomplished.

May this be your best year yet.

60

BUY, SELL, OR HOLD?

CONSIDER WHICH PATH FORWARD IS THE RIGHT ONE FOR YOU

A s the telephone answering service industry continues to contract amid a sellers' market, it leaves many wondering what the future looks like as they contemplate their long-term strategy.

There are three general scenarios that apply to most situations: buy, sell, or hold.

Buy: Some large players continue their buying spree. While they've snatched up most of the good deals, many attractive targets still exist.

The objectives of this strategy vary. For some, it's the cash flow. For others, it's pursuing greater economies of scale. And for still others, it's the basic driving force that bigger is better. Regardless, these folks continue to make acquisitions in pursuit of their core objective.

Three essential steps exist for those who buy answering services. First is the ability to strike a sound deal. The second is to orchestrate a smooth transition. And third, which some people skip, is opti-mizing the acquisition for maximum financial results.

Sell: Some answering services wonder if they should sell. This is a legitimate question, especially given the sellers' market and the competition that exists across North America. Selling could make for a smart exit strategy. (See chapter 65, "What's Your Exit Strategy?" at the end of this section.)

For answering services pursuing this scenario, the goal is to do everything possible to make your answering service attractive to a potential buyer. This means maximizing EBITDA (earnings before interest, taxes, depreciation, and amortization).

Items include maximizing the profitability of each account, eliminating unnecessary spending, and removing owner perks from the equation. Not only will each step made to improve EBITDA increase the sales price, but it will also increase profitability.

Hold: The remaining group of answering services is interested in neither buying nor selling. They want to maintain their operation at its current size or to grow organically through sales and marketing.

Although there are many strategies to allow this to work successfully, the most promising one is to implement a niche and then pursue it for growth and profitability. (See chapter 63, "Does Your TAS Have a Niche?" later in this section.)

This niche could be a certain segment of the market, a unique way of onboarding or serving clients, or a convincing marketing vision that sells the company image as much as its service. Many answering services are successfully pursuing this course, proving that it can be done. But don't copy their specific strategy. Instead, tweak it to make your own.

Moving Forward: Think strategically and move intentionally to produce a successful outcome. But you must first pick the one that's right for you.

61

RETHINK YOUR TAS FOR THE LONG TERM

APPLY YOUR EXPERIENCES OF THE PAST TO CHART YOUR FUTURE COURSE

I 'm a fan of fine-tuning processes and paradigms over time. I prefer incremental changes to a complete overhaul. Yet some situations require significant correction.

Here are key areas that warrant serious contemplation.

Location: Since its inception over a century ago, telephone answering services have operated from a single location. Although the concept of remote agents has been an option since the late 80s, only more recently has the promise of a distributed workforce become a viable consideration.

With few exceptions, answering service leaders hold a firm perspective on which setting—centrally located or dispersed—is the best. Many understandably prefer a centralized workforce.

Now, however, is an ideal time to push aside this proven, preferred way of doing business to at least *consider* the alternative. This distributed model can work from dispersed offices, employees' homes, or both. The centralized location, and all its associated costs, can become relegated to history.

Platform Type: Another more recent development is that answering services now have two platform configurations to choose from: on-premise or off-site, which is effectively a subscription service, sometimes known as SaaS (software as a service). Both have their advantages and drawbacks. There is no universally right answer, but there is a right answer for *your* service and what you want to accomplish.

Take a serious look at the strengths and weaknesses of your current platform configuration. Contrast this with the opposite situation and see which one is the better strategic move for the long term. Consider stability, flexibility, cost, and future potential. There is much to contemplate.

Staffing: Relating to location and platform type is the staffing paradigm you want to pursue. Many managers desire to see their staff at work each day or at least be able to work some of their shifts at the main answering service location. This requires that employees live within driving distance of the service.

This requirement, however, severely limits your labor pool. What if agents could do *all* their work remotely? What if you could fully train them at a distance? Then your potential labor pool expands geographically, as well as allowing you to consider nontraditional workers, such as the homebound but otherwise qualified candidate.

Management: Make no mistake. It's hard for most to manage a distributed workforce. What worked well in person seldom translates to a dispersed team working from multiple locations. This may be the hardest transition of all to make. It requires learning, implementing, and mastering the ability to manage from a distance. Most find it challenging, but it may prove a rewarding pursuit.

Think strategically about these wide-ranging, future-enhancing changes to your telephone answering service.

Moving Forward: Prepare now to better deal with the future. Regardless of what happens tomorrow, you'll be glad you prepared for it today.

62

HAVING A DISTRIBUTED WORKFORCE

KEY CONSIDERATIONS FOR A DECENTRALIZED TEAM

W hether you already have a decentralized operation or are just in the thinking stage, here are some areas to address:

Technical Logistics: The first step in allowing staff to work from home is the technical aspect of getting them connected. This starts with a stable internet connection and adequate computer resources in each home. Consider the glitches and challenges that could occur and anticipate your response to them now instead of when a problem occurs.

HR and Legal Considerations: Aside from the technical and management issues, there are the human resources considerations and legal aspects of having staff work from home, even from another state—or country. Update your employee handbook and procedural manuals to reflect this. Review your insurance coverage to make sure it addresses a distributed, home-based workforce. Consult with a labor attorney to make sure you have the needed protection and adequate resources in the event an off-site employee goes rogue.

Platform: If you have a premise-based system, consider moving to the cloud. This will best facilitate remote staff and provide maximum flexibility. In addition, an off-premise solution removes equipment from your building, which brings up the next point.

Facility: As staff moves off-site, you will require less space in your building. If you lease, this means you can scale back or cut your rent. If you own the building, you can either sell it or lease unused space to other businesses. Taken to an extreme, if everyone works from home, you no longer need a physical office.

Sales: Consider how much of your sales occurs online versus how much results from in-person meetings. Looking forward, expect that more local prospects will not need physical interaction with your sales team. Strive to reach the point where all sales efforts can occur from a distance.

Business Support Functions: Though much of the work-at-home focus has been on answering service agents, explore how you can extend that concept to non-operational staff. What if everyone worked from home? What are the risks . . . and benefits?

Remote Management: Overseeing a distributed workforce challenges most people. It requires a different approach than with in-person management. How can you maintain oversight and control to produce the best results?

Stay Connected: As you send more of your staff home to work, consider what steps you can take to stay connected with each other, and engaged in work. What can you do to counter feelings of isolation? Seek creative ways to maintain morale, effectiveness, and efficiency when physical, in-person interaction doesn't exist or is minimal. Consider conference calls, video meetings, and online interaction—both formal and informal.

Moving Forward: Having a distributed workforce is a formidable challenge to master, but you must at least consider it. Though not essential, decentralization can provide a strategic advantage.

63

DOES YOUR TAS HAVE A NICHE?

CONSIDER PURSUING A SPECIALIST STRATEGY

I t used to be that most telephone answering services functioned as a generalist—serving all clients in all industries. But might a niche strategy be what's needed in today's marketplace?

Niche Considerations: A huge answering service niche is the healthcare industry. Other possible niches include property management and transportation. There are also regional opportunities, such as with the logging, shipping, oil and natural gas, farming, tourist, and entertainment industries.

The niche a telephone answering service elects to pursue should hinge on the size of that market and the answering service's connection and affinity with that industry. Never pursue a promising niche if your company lacks experience serving it or if it bores you.

Developing services specifically geared toward a particular industry establishes expertise and increases proficiency that's unobtainable by a generalist answering service. Increased efficiency will result. This provides the option to charge less, improve profitability, or both.

Find Your Niche: There's nothing wrong with being a generalist, but if you are a broad-based telephone answering service, you might decide to grow your business by pursuing strategic niches. But how do you determine which niches to pursue?

Look at the accounts you currently handle. Do you see any trends or groups? Poll your staff. Ask them which accounts they like and why. Also consider items such as profitability, customer service needs, and payment history. These factors often vary by industry or subgroup. If so, they should be easy to identify.

Ideally, you want to pursue a niche you're already good at, you've proven yourself in, and your staff enjoys and serves well. Also, seek a niche that will pay profitable fees, doesn't overtax your support team, and pays on time. Though it's unlikely to find a market segment that satisfies all six considerations, seek to match as many items as possible.

Diversify Your Niche: Pursuing a niche, however, is akin to the adage of "putting all your eggs in one basket." The key is to diversify by developing multiple niches. After establishing yourself in one niche, pursue a second, and then add a third.

Most times, three niches is the minimum number. This keeps an economic downturn in one niche from financially devastating your TAS. If one niche tanks, you have the other two to prop up your operation and maintain some stability. Of course, this assumes each niche represents a comparable percentage of business. A general guide is that it's unwise to derive more than half of your business from any one industry or market.

Moving Forward: When pursued strategically, niches can provide a means for growth and stability. Only you can decide if a niche strategy is right for your answering service. But if it is, be intentional about it.

64

DEALING WITH OWNER LIFE CYCLE CHANGES

PREPARING FOR THE NEXT GENERATION

A problem faced by telephone answering service owners, like all business owners, is addressing life cycle changes: dealing with shifting priorities as they age.

Scaling Back: While some people may have both the drive and ability to run a business for the rest of their lives, most get to a point where they want to scale back: not handling day-to-day issues, taking longer vacations, semi-retiring, or not working at all. These are all forms of letting go.

Yet letting go is often hard for someone who sacrificed much to launch or grow a business. As the longtime owner, you may make every key decision and oversee all activities.

If there is a family member or key employee interested in taking over the business, this may be the best solution to help you achieve your goals, provided there is enough time to make an orderly transition.

Passing the Baton: Most family businesses don't successfully transfer to the second generation, and only about 15 percent make it to the third.

A likely factor is that the second generation, who didn't sacrifice to launch the business and see it through the lean years, lacks the resilience to persevere. Another reason is that problems occur if parents hand the business over too quickly to adult children who lack needed experience.

Some entrepreneurial parents attempt to avoid these problems by making their successor children start at an entry-level position and work their way up the organization. But this fast-track status often backfires, causing resentment from non-relative staff who may be more qualified, better educated, or have longer tenure.

To circumvent this, some founders require their children to earn a college degree and put in time at another company to learn essential skills before joining the family business. Although this approach may offer the greatest chance for success, it isn't a sure-fire strategy.

If your goal is to pass your TAS on to your children, be intentional about it and plan. Don't leave business succession to chance, or you may end up like most family-owned businesses that fail to pass the baton to their kids successfully.

Selling the Operation: Many TAS owners, however, find themselves in a position where their children, other family members, or employees don't want the business—or aren't prepared to run it. Then they opt for the alternative: they sell the business to an outsider.

Moving Forward: Carefully consider all the options and make an informed decision after taking time to determine the best choice for your situation. Whatever you do, don't put things off and be forced to make a rash decision.

65

WHAT'S YOUR EXIT STRATEGY?

CONSIDER PASSING YOUR TAS TO YOUR KIDS OR A KEY EMPLOYEE

I f you own a telephone answering service, you spend a lot of time thinking about the future—or at least you should. And if you're not the owner but a key employee, you should also consider what's ahead.

Future considerations for owners may include growth, acquisition, or new technology. When you think about the future, however, you should also plan how to move forward. There are five options to consider when it's time to scale back or retire.

1. Sell to Family: Look to your family for people who could take over your answering service and buy it from you. If you sell to a family member, make sure he or she understands the industry and knows how to run the business. Identify these potential people and groom them to take over.

2. Sell to a Key Employee: Another option is to sell your operation to a key employee. They know your business and the industry. They've proven themselves.

Alternately you can sell to a group of employees. By converting your business to an ESOP (Employee Stock Ownership Plan) you can make an orderly transition, allowing your employees to have an ownership stake.

3. Sell to Another Company: Aside from family and employees, you can also look to sell to another answering service or to an outside investor. Going this route may produce the highest selling price, but it might be at the sacrifice of your legacy, staff, or clients. Balance the pros and cons.

4. Work Until the End: By intention, or sometimes not, some business owners continue in their role until the day they die. This eliminates the need for an exit strategy, but it passes the burden on to their heirs. If you decide to do this, do them a favor and leave them with a transition plan.

5. Shut Down the Business: Some small answering services assume their business has no value, so they close their doors. There's no reason to do that. Though you may not have a big enough operation to attract high-dollar buyers, your accounts do have value, and other services are eager to buy them for a fair price.

Tips for Key Employees: This discussion focuses on answering service owners, but what if you're a manager? Consider these scenarios and envision how you can be part of the business owner's exit strategy. This may involve a direct discussion, or it may require a subtler approach.

Either way, the potential exists for you to become an answering service owner. Then you'll one day need to form your own exit strategy.

Moving Forward: The key for a successful exit is to make a plan and then work your plan.

THE NEXT STEP
FORM AN ACTION PLAN

I n this book, we've covered sixty-five discussions—grouped in nine sections—on how to move forward with your telephone answering service. That's a lot to consider. Some items might not apply to your situation, while others will seem trivial. But give serious consideration to what remains.

Perhaps you've kept a running list of action steps as you read through this book. Or maybe your first pass left your mind swirling with too many ideas to handle. Regardless of where you're at, it's time to act. If you don't, this book will amount to little more than a thought-provoking exercise.

If you know exactly what your next step is, that's great. Now make it happen.

If, however, you don't yet have that clarity, reread the book with intention. Or you can skim it, considering the *moving forward* sections at the end of each chapter. As you do this, list all the steps you think warrant attention. Just make a list. Don't judge its viability or evaluate its priority.

Once you have your possible action steps listed, go through and group them. Place them in three categories: nice, important, and critical. Set aside the *nice* items and the *important* items for later.

Focus on the *critical* items. Now rank them.

What is the single most significant item on your *critical* list? This is the first task on your action plan. Now rank the other *critical* items in order of importance underneath your number one priority.

Now move forward with intention, tackling your number one priority. When done—and only when done—move to the second item on your list. Then work through the other items on your *critical* list, one at a time.

Once you've worked through the *critical* list—which could take months or even years—repeat the process for the items on your *important* list. Again, tackle them one at a time. When they're done, move to the items on your *nice* list.

And if you worry you might never get to your *important* list, let alone your *nice* list, see what you can delegate to other people on your staff. That will get them involved and take some pressure off you.

With a vision for how to proceed in place, now move forward with intention. May it bring you both success and satisfaction.

~

If you liked *The Profitable Answering Service,* please leave a review online. Your review will help others discover this book and encourage them to read it too.

Thank you.

ABOUT PETER LYLE DEHAAN

Peter Lyle DeHaan, PhD, is a call center veteran. His lifetime of experience includes leading and managing a multi-location telephone answering service, employment with an industry vendor, call center consulting, and publishing call center periodicals and books.

Learn more at PeterLyleDeHaan.com.

BOOKS BY PETER LYLE DEHAAN

Call Center Success Series

Healthcare Call Center Essentials

Call Center Connections

How to Start a Telephone Answering Service

The Profitable Answering Service

The Healthy Medical Call Center (due out in 2026)

Sticky Success Strategies

Sticky Customer Service

Sticky Sales and Marketing

Sticky Leadership and Management

Sticky Living

Academic Research

The Telephone Answering Service Industry

Turning a Telephone Answering Service into a Call Center

Other Books

Successful Author FAQs

For a complete, up-to-date list of Peter's books, go to
PeterLyleDeHaan.com/books.

www.ingramcontent.com/pod-product-compliance
Lightning Source LLC
Chambersburg PA
CBHW071211210326
41597CB00016B/1765